Fuse It

A Continuing Journey in Kiln Worked Glass

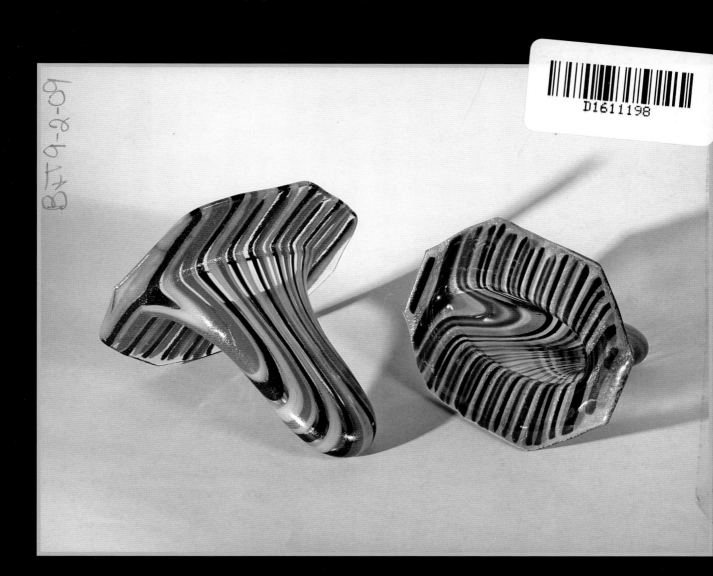

Wardell
PUBLICATIONS INC

Cataloging in Publication Data

Kaiser, Petra, 1960-

  Fuse It: A Continuing Journey in Kiln Worked Glass

Author: Petra Kaiser; Text editor: Randy Wardell

Includes index

ISBN-13: 978-0-919985-52-0

ISBN-10: 0-919985-52-1

  1. Glass fusing. I. Wardell, Randy A. (Randy Allan), 1954- II. Title. III. Title: Fuse It.

TT298.K348 2006   748.2028   C2006-902914-8

Printed in Thailand by Phongwarin Printing Ltd.

Published simultaneously in Canada and USA

E-mail: info@wardellpublications.com

Website: www.wardellpublications.com

Fuse It

A Continuing Journey in Kiln Worked Glass

Author & Designer
Petra Kaiser

Text Editor
Randy Wardell

Fabrication Assistance
Wolfgang Kaiser

Cover Design
Christine Arleij

Photography
Wolfgang Kaiser & Randy Wardell

Book Layout & Typography
Randy Wardell & Carole Wardell

Author's Acknowledgements

I would like to thank Carole and Randy Wardell as well as my husband Wolfgang since without them this 'Fuse It' book would not exist. The support of literally hundreds of glass enthusiasts offering their advice, challenging me in our workshops and inspiring me with the confidence to keep on working. I appreciate the fused glass and tool manufacturers for continuing to develop innovative products and especially for keeping me up to date on their new products and technologies. I would like to thank all those who provided an opportunity for Wolfgang and I to teach in some of the most beautiful locations, not only here in the United States but also in several international venues. I would like to thank our patrons and art collectors for their support of our artwork. And finally I would like to mention three people in particular, Shigemi Ohkubo a wonderful glass artist and her husband Yoshio Ohkubo for giving us the opportunity to show and sell our work in Japan and also Tiite Baquero who is famous for his Worldwide Peace Marker Project, thanks for being a friend, a mentor and for collaborating with us on our first four dimensional works.

Published by

Wardell
PUBLICATIONS INC

River Valley District Library
214 South Main, P.O. Box 10
Port Byron, Illinois 61275
309-523-3440 10/02/09

To receive our electronic newsletter or to send suggestions please contact us

by e-mail: info@wardellpublications.com or visit our Website: www.wardellpublications.com

A Message from the Author

Our TA (teacher's assistant) Cleopetra is shown here watching over our classroom from her chair in the studio crows nest.

You may already know that my husband Wolfgang and I are the distributors of Kaiser Lee Board, a kiln shelf and mold material that is at the core of many of the innovative projects we have developed. When I have an idea for a new project I get a real thrill out of finding the most uncomplicated, economical and trouble-free way to achieve beautiful kiln worked glass art. More often than not it's Kaiser Lee Board that enables me to accomplish what I'm striving for. In fact some projects would be almost impossible to do if I didn't have Kaiser Lee Board. I have had an inner struggle while writing this book. I definitely do not want my readers to be left with the impression that this is a promo piece for Kaiser Lee Board at the exclusion of other alternatives. To me, it is nothing more than the medium that enables me to achieve the effects and shapes that I'm striving for successfully and hassle free.

I am proud to say that I have an active teaching program at my studio, training dozens of students each year. In the past I would start my classes with the more traditional fusing techniques using kiln wash releases on clay kiln shelves, slumping into ceramic molds and casting with firebrick dams. My intention was to educate them by presenting the whole picture and to try to remain politically neutral while mixing my teaching assignment with our KL board distribution business. After the class has completed a few projects in the traditional way, I show them some techniques using Kaiser Lee Board. That is when I receive the surprising reaction of "Why in the world are you teaching us the old way when you know an easier, more versatile and successful way". To be honest I didn't have a good answer for that. I was trying to give my students all the options but what they really wanted was to have fun fusing with the least amount of problems. Sometimes even the best of intention can lead you down the wrong path.

This book is truly an extension of my first book 'Introduction to Glass Fusing' I have received literally hundreds of e-mails from readers telling me they use it frequently as a reference book. It is my hope that the projects lessons and techniques presented in 'Fuse It' will stimulate the same outcome.

Have fun, get inspired and get your kiln fired up!

Keep it hot!
petra

Author Contact Information

Kaiser Glass Design Studio
3732 SE 21st Place,
Cape Coral, FL 33904 USA
Phone: 239-540-1137
E-mail: petra@kaiserlee.com
Website: www.kaiserlee.com

Table Of Contents

Introduction

Lessons & Instruction

Showcase Galleries

A dichroic cabochon pendant with matching beads on a sterling silver necklace chain. The simple earring is from project 1 'Jewelry Ensemble Part 3 - Earrings With Fine Silver, on page 32.

Introduction

A Brief History Of Time

In my first book, 'Introduction to Glass Fusing' I highlighted some ancient history about art glass. This time I would like to deal with some much more recent history - the period of time since I personally entered the glass fusing world in 1996, until today - a very 'brief history of time' indeed.

"An illustrated tutorial on the techniques of art glass fusing. Filled with easy to follow step-by-step photos, useful tip sidebars and complete project instructions."

Introduction to

Glass Fusing

PROJECT-BY-PROJECT GUIDED LESSONS
A Comprehensive Guide to Glass Fusing Techniques

by Petra Kaiser

'Introduction to Glass Fusing' by Petra Kaiser was first published in 2003. It is an illustrated guide on the tools, materials and techniques for crafters who are beginning to explore the art glass fusing.

I was living in the town of Darmstadt, Germany in 1985 where I dabbled a bit in traditional stained glass and quickly discovered that it was really not my cup of tea. I just didn't like the idea of being confined to a create a specific size, in addition to the requirement for very accurate glass cutting, careful grinding and shaping, followed by meticulous fabrication. It simply was not the way I preferred to work.

Fusing Class Sounds Interesting

My husband Wolfgang and I moved to the United States in 1996 and after a few months I discovered the Art Studio of Cape Coral, Florida. The studio offered classes in drawing, painting and pottery plus two classes with the word 'glass' in their title. One class was stained glass and the other was glass fusing. To be honest I wasn't sure what 'fusing' was exactly but it sounded kind of interesting to my German ear. I thought it might be the English word for glass blowing or at least lamp working, so I enrolled. To my surprise and eventual delight - I found out that you could create art from glass in a kiln. By the end of the six week class, I was hooked.

I knew we were fortunate to have local fusing classes plus readily available fusible glass, kilns, equipment and other necessary supplies but it never occurred to me that our area might be an exception. With the benefit of hindsight I can now recognize the signs, for example the absence of fused glass artists at craft shows, the fact that nobody seemed to know what 'glass fusing' was (including myself just a short time earlier) and galleries seemed just a little too eager to accept our early fused glass pieces as 'artwork' for display in their showrooms.

We soon discovered a unique fiberboard product that we now call Kaiser Lee Board and began to distribute it in 1999. Our first commercial showing of KL board was at a dealer weekend for one of our distributors and then we exhibited at the Glass Art Show in Long Beach, California. At each event visitors were very interested in our display of fused glass pieces created with KL board molds. It did not take us long to realize that we needed to modify our greeting for show buyers to ask, "Are you currently doing any glass fusing?" The vast majority answered, "No, but it sure looks interesting" or "I am considering it - please tell me more."

I'll never forget a conversation I had with Randy Wardell (now my Editor & Publisher) at that first dealer weekend. I asked him, "You have so many books on stained glass, why don't you have any on glass fusing?" His response was, "I have thought about it but I am not sure there are enough hobby glass fusers to support one at this time". However glass fusing was quickly gaining popularity and continued to attract enthusiastic followers. In 2001 Randy approached me with a proposal to publish an entry-level technique book on glass fusing - if I would write one. I was very flattered especially since I'd never written a book before. So, without knowing what I was getting into, I accepted the challenge.

From Bathing to Sweating

Two years later with lots of help from my husband Wolfgang and also from Carole and Randy Wardell, the book was introduced in July of 2003 at the Glass Art Show in Chicago, Illinois. For six months I was bathing in my newfound fame. I received many e-mails from readers telling me how much they were enjoying my book. Then people started to ask for more and I remembered the promise I had made in that first book that we would 'talk about this or that in a future book'. So it wasn't long before I was done with 'bathing' and found myself back in the 'sweat shop' creating new projects and writing text for this sequel book.

We taught classes and exhibited at the Glass Art and Bead Expo in Las Vegas in 2004 (and every year since). What an exciting time to walk the show floor, talk to students and meet other glass artists involved in a variety of warm glass disciplines. I know I was not the only one at that show in 2004 who noticed a clear shift in the quality and variety of fused glass artwork. Manufacturers were introducing new and innovative equipment, tools, glass and other products specifically for fusing. Artists were developing new techniques and everyone was inspiring each another with inventive work that would invariably ignite the next idea.

It was and continues to be an exciting time to be involved in this ever-expanding art form. I believe it is of the utmost importance for us to share our knowledge and enthusiasm and to encourage artists and crafters in all walks of life to join our 'Continuing Journey in Kiln Worked Glass'.

This elegant but simple fused corner assembly is glued to a beveled mirror. See page 36 for another 'Wall Mirror' project.

Materials & Supplies

This parts bin rack is a great organizer for all our frit, powders, stringers, zigzag sticks and so much more.

A collection of rulers and straight edges, putty knife, pens and carving tools.

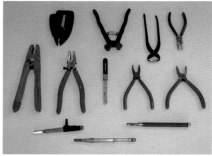

Glass tools, including 3 glasscutters (at bottom), running, breaking & grozing pliers and mosaic nippers (top center).

This is not an entry-level book so we are going to assume that you already have the basic tools, equipment, glass & supplies that every fusing studio needs. Obviously there is no way for us to know exactly what you have and don't have and that is why we are providing this list and description of every item that we used to create the projects presented in this book.

It is not required to memorize this list, however it would be a good idea to read through it and make a note of anything that you don't have. As you're reading the project instructions you will find statements like, "Use a small putty knife (or old kitchen knife) to cut and remove the oval from the center of your KL board". To do that project you would need the items mentioned to complete the step. If you're not familiar with any of the tools, simply take a look back to this section for more information.

You certainly don't need everything on this list. Much will depend on which projects you choose to work on. Many of the items are available in numerous model types and styles. As always, it's a good idea to ask your friendly local fusing supplier for their recommendation before making your purchase.

Project Planning & Organization

- Pattern Making: paper, ruler, pencil, fine marker, scissors, craft knife
- Glass Storage: custom glass racks, a Morton Glass Caddy, assorted plastic containers i.e. plastic parts bins (for small glass pieces, stringers & other components) sturdy cardboard boxes,
- General Storage: shelving, pegboard racks, cupboards, etc.

Glass Preparation Tools & Equipment

- Worktable: for glass cutting and pre-firing preparation
- Glass Cutting Surface: Morton surface that provides pockets to catch small glass chips, solid cutting surface for smaller pieces, e.g. soft tile board (the type used for drop ceilings)
- Permanent Markers: (to draw on glass) black, silver &/or white
- Glass Cutting & Shaping: glasscutter, breaking pliers, mosaic cutters, strip-cutter, Morton Glass Shop
- Assembly & Manipulation: tweezers (with bent nose), putty knife - stainless steel blade 1" (2.5 cm) & 3" (7.6 cm), kitchen (butter) knife, stainless steel rake for hot glass combing (see next page bottom right)
- Jeweler's Tools: flush cutters (wire cutters), needle nosed pliers, round and flat pliers, jewelers hammer and anvil, wire brush, polishing paper, lapidary tumbler with stainless steel shot

Assembly & Cleaning

- Adhesives (for pre-fire assembly): Hotline Fusers Glue, Thompson Klyr Fire™, Bullseye Glasstac™, white bond glue

- Adhesives (for final assembly): E-6000™, Bond 527™, Triolyse™, Gorilla Glue™ (does not dry clear), Mirror Mastic, UV Glue (for translucent glass only)

- Soft Cloth: you will need a supply of fabric cloths to use for cleaning at various stages in the fusing process. I like to use cotton dishcloths but many fusers use old towels, T-shirts or similar types of cotton material, cut into assorted sizes

- Plastic Wash Basin: approximately 10" x 14" x 5" deep (25 x 36 x 13 cm deep) this will be used to soak and wash your glass components prior to firing

- Plastic Trash Bucket (aka 'Dunk Bucket'): 8" x 14" x 12" deep (20 x 36 x 30 cm deep) or larger if you are working on big items, used to soak and wash your glass projects after firing to remove fiber release materials

- Cleaner Solutions: Isopropyl Alcohol (rubbing alcohol), dish washing detergent, Goof Off™ (used to remove sticky residue)

Cleaning supplies and adhesives.

Safety & Protection Supplies

- Eye Protection: glasses, goggles, full face shield

- Breathing Protection: dust mask, respirator

- Hand Protection: hi-temp gloves (for kiln working), cut resistant gloves (for glass), vinyl gloves (for chemicals & mold materials)

- Clothing Protection: shop apron or lab coat

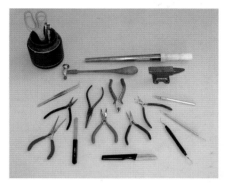

Jewelers' tools including ring mandrel (top right), hammer & anvil, plus assorted pliers, cutters, files and picks.

Power Tools and Accessories

- Glass Grinder: table top machine designed to grind and shape glass

- Grinding Head Diamond: standard grit the size to fit your glass grinder

- Drilling Head Diamond: 1/8" & 1/4" (3 & 6 mm) for grinder

- High-speed Rotary Tool (Drill): minimum 20,000 rpm

- Diamond Coated Drill Bits for Rotary Tool: assorted sizes: 5/64" (2 mm), 5/32" (4 mm), 1/4" (6 mm), 5/16" (8 mm), 3/8" (10 mm)

- Shallow Plastic 'cafeteria' Tray: approximately 10" x 14" x 3/4" deep (25 x 36 x 2 cm deep) used when drilling holes in glass

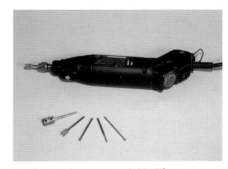

High-speed rotary tool (drill) minimum 20,000 rpm plus 5 diamond coated drill bits.

Specialized Materials

- Lamp Parts (candelabra light kit) including: 1 Threaded nipple - 3/4" (2 cm), 2 Brass lock nuts, 1 Brass washer, 2 Rubber washers, 1 Mini-base bulb socket, 1 Power cord with in-line switch (hardware store supplies)

- Clock Movement: threaded shaft at least 3/8" long, battery operated

- Stainless Steel Fasteners: 1/4" (6.4 mm) round head bolts 1 1/2" (4 cm) long, 1/4" (6 mm) hex nuts, 1/4" (6 mm) acorn nuts

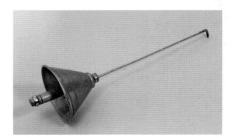

Rake tool with wooden handle and heat shield used to put swirls in the surface of molten glass. See 'Hot Streak Cast Vase' project on page 72.

Glass for Fusing

One of the glass racks in my studio containing full and partial sheets of compatible glass. Whenever I cut a sheet I write the COE number on all pieces using a permanent marker before placing them back in the rack.

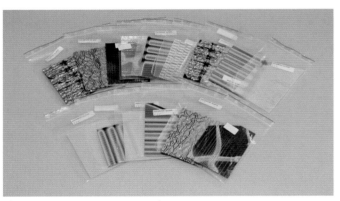

A rainbow of dichroic glass pieces shown here individually packed in zip-lock bags for easy selection and purchase.

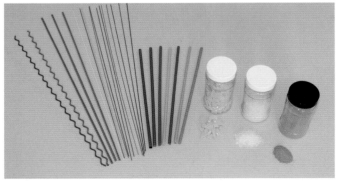

This selection from left to right; dichroic zigzag sticks, noodle & spaghetti stringers, 'pencil-thick' rods, frit in coarse, medium & fine.

In glass fusing terminology, 'fusing compatible glass' refers to any glass that has been determined by the manufacturer to be compatible with any other glass sharing the same COE. Compatible is defined as, glass that can be melted (fused) together and will be free from stress when cooled. I provided an extensive explanation of what fusible glass is and how it is identified in my first book 'Introduction to Glass Fusing'. For this book I only want to remind you that it is imperative that all glass used in any single project including frit and powders must have the same COE number. It's fine to mix glass from different manufacturers - so long as you match the COE's. I cannot stress how important it is for you to devise a filing system or other method to keep glass of different COE separated in your studio. You cannot tell the COE of a glass by looking at it and you don't know if a sheet is 'tested compatible' unless it has the manufacturers sticker on it. (See Hot Tip on page 11) for some ideas to help you organize and file your fusing glass.

What is COE Anyway?

It does not mean 'Cash On Exit' (even though that may feel like what's happening sometimes), no, it really mean's Co-efficient Of Expansion. This number is a manufacturer's code that refers to the rate and amount of expansion and contraction of a given material (in this case glass) when heated and cooled. If you want to learn more about the mesmerizing subject of COE, you will find an abundance of information on the fusing glass manufacturers Internet sites. The fact is all you really need to know is the COE number of every glass component you intend to combine in any single project - keep them all the same and you're good to go!

When casting big pieces of glass it is best to use the largest chunks possible in the mold to reduce the incidence of air bubbles. These pieces of casting billets can be broken up into smaller chunks.

Confetti shards are paper-thin pieces of glass that can be sprinkled on your fuse project to add a splash of color, shading, hazing or blending. See page 49 to learn a method to make your own shards.

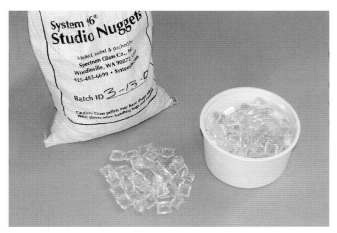

These studio nuggets are crystal-clear glass pillows approximately 3/4" (2 cm) square. They are available in clear only and are perfect for casting projects.

This product is clear glass cullett. It is basically crushed glass with sizes running from powder to as much as 3/4" (2 cm) and is used primarily for casting projects.

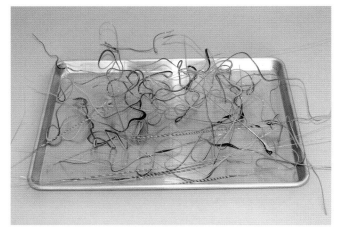

This tray full of 'Gestural Strings Of Glass' was made using our flow system kiln set-up. See Project 14 on page 84 to find out how much fun it is to make your own.

HotTip If you have both COE 90 and COE 96 glass (or any other COE) in your studio, it is critical to clearly mark them and keep them separated. One effective method is to use color-coded small dot stickers (available from any office supply store). Place a blue dot on all COE 90 glass and red dots on COE 96 (or any color you like) or use a permanent marker to write '90' or '96' on every piece you have (this is how I do it). Whenever you cut a larger sheet into smaller pieces, place the correct color dot (or number code) onto each and every leftover piece before storing them. For smaller pieces, set up scrap bins with the COE number on them and then place your scraps into the correct COE bin.

Kilns & Controllers

There is no question that the kiln is the heart of every fusing studio. Actually since most studios and many hobby fusers have 2 or more kilns, I guess you could say fusing is a 'multiple' heart operation. There are dozens of different kilns available and kiln manufacturers introduce new models on a regular basis. It is not possible to describe all the options, styles, sizes and shapes that you will find. Instead let's take a look at the various alternatives that you'll need to consider when you decide to make a kiln purchase.

Chamber Size

Many of the projects in this book require a kiln with a mid-sized chamber. A number of the projects could be adapted for a smaller kiln but you'll need to make a decision on the size and types of items you intend to create on a regular basis before purchasing a kiln. If your chief interest is in making jewelry components or accent tiles then a kiln with an interior

This is a view of our studio kiln room showing our 'pride & joy' box kiln with a firing chamber of 28" x 42" x 12" deep (70 x 105 x 30 cm). It can hold several projects at once - or one very large project. (See inside this kiln on page 25). The digital controller (notice the small box on the right side of the kiln) can store several firing schedules, making set-up and running the kiln a breeze once it is loaded and ready to go.

dimension of 6" to 9" (15 to 23 cm) will work just fine. However a medium sized kiln from 14" to 20" (35 to 51 cm) would be a better purchase if you plan to fuse and shape projects like the ones found in this book. You may want to consider a professional style kiln in the 24" (61 cm) size, or an oval kiln measuring 20" x 30" (51 to 76 cm). You will also find professional kilns starting at 20" (51 cm) square or rectangles 28" x 42" (72 x 107 cm). This is the kiln size I have in my studio shown in the photo above.

Most of my students start out by purchasing one of the smaller box kilns with a chamber size of 9" x 9" (23 x 23 cm). Once they have gained some experience and are ready to move to the next level they have a better idea of the kind of projects they want to pursue. Most find that they continue to use the smaller kiln for jewelry and for making components that will be incorporated into larger projects. Be sure to check out the 'Compon It' projects in this book, starting on page 80 for interesting suggestions for a smaller kiln.

Electrical Considerations

Kilns have a variety of electrical requirements. You will need to consider into account the type of electrical feed that you have in the workroom where you intend to install the kiln. It is very important that the voltage, amperage and wiring are matched to the requirement of the kiln and that it complies with the electrical code in your area. Be sure to consult a professional electrician. In the interest of safety the kiln must to be set away from all flammable surfaces and must be properly wired.

This is a high voltage electrical outlet most often required when installing larger kilns. You'll need an electrician to run one of these special circuits.

Shape and Lid Position

Kilns are available in a range of sizes and depths and each is obtainable in oval, square, rectangle and round (actually 6, 7 or 8 sided). Kilns can be top loading, where the lid is positioned on the topside with a hinged opening (see kiln top right photo), some models have removable lids (no hinge) and still others are hinged at the bottom (called clamshell opening). Front loading kilns open more like a microwave oven to give access to the firing chamber (see front loading kiln in photo top right). As you might expect there are even more elaborate models. One kiln style called a 'bell type' are often custom made. They can be large enough to fuse an entire entrance door in one piece. The lid on these kilns is lifted vertically off the table using wires and pulleys, then the table is rolled out from under the lid on a rail system. This gives the artist access to load the large chamber by walking around the table on all sides. Each model has its advantages, be sure to ask the sales associate at your local store for more details.

Front loading square kiln above left and a 10 sided top loader at right.

Heating Elements

Larger electric fusing kilns have heating elements in the sidewalls as well as in the top (usually the lid) . However some models have elements in the sidewalls only and others have them in the top only. Again there are advantages to each so ask your fusing supply center for assistance.

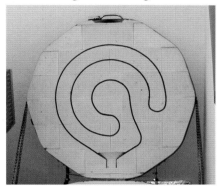

This top loading kiln has heating elements in the lid and in the sides.

Kiln Controllers

You will need a way to turn the kiln on and off but it's not always that simple. Smaller kilns have a dial type controller switch with several power level positions and a pyrometer (hi-temp thermometer) to enable the operator to determine the various firing stages. These work well but require the operator to pay careful attention to the firing schedule. A kitchen style timer is good to set also. The only practical way to conduct a firing in a larger kiln is with the assistance of a digital controller. It can be programmed to automatically run the temperature up at a specified rate, hold a specific temperature for a set period of time and then allow the kiln to cool at the required rate and soak for proper annealing.

This controller is designed for kilns that run on standard household current.

Some controllers have to be programmed using your own firing schedules (or use the schedules in this book), while other controllers come pre-programmed with 5 or 6 of the most common schedules. The good news is you only have to enter each schedule once and the controller will memorize it so you can recall it anytime you need it.

Which kiln is the right one for you?

The selection and purchase of your kiln is vital and many factors must be taken into consideration. Consult with other fusers and do some research at the websites of the various kiln manufacturers to get as much information as you can. Your kiln is an important and major investment that necessitates some determined research.

This small box kiln has been adapted to make flow stringers - see page 84.

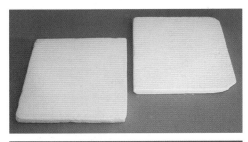

Assorted kiln shelves top photo; KL board with shelf release (left) and uncoated (right), lower photo; mullite clay (left) and Alumina Silica Fiberboard (right).

ProTip

A Clear Distinction Between Draping & Slumping

Some fusers use 'slumping' as a general term to describe both of these processes, but we like to make a clear distinction between the two. **'Draping'** glass means that you place the glass on top of a mold form and allow the outer perimeter of the glass to fall and 'drape' around the mold. In many cases you'll get a more free-formed shape (see 'test drape 1 & 2' on page 59). It is possible to control the outcome of a drape by strategically designing the blank to match the mold (see Pendant Chandelier on pages 58 & 59). **'Slumping'** refers to the technique of forming the glass by allowing the center of the glass blank to drop into a mold. We used a KL board slump mold to form the platters and bowls in the gallery on pages 76 & 77. You will also find dozens of clay slump molds available to form plates, platters, bowls and more.

Kiln Shelves

Mullite clay: The most common shelf used for glass fusing is the clay kiln shelf made from Mullite clay. These 1/2" (1.2 cm) thick shelves are available from all kiln supply distributors and are usually 1" or 2" (2.5 to 5 cm) smaller then the inside dimension of the kiln.

Alumina Silica 'Fiberboard': Fiberboard shelves offer a distinct advantage over traditional clay since this material does not absorb or retain heat, helping to ensure a more even heat distribution (see The Secret To Successful Firing on page 19). There are currently a number of fiberboard variations available in the glass fusing market, Kaiser Lee Board, Duraboard™ and Fiberfrax™ to name three. There are significant preparation and use differences between these products, be sure to read 'Kaiser Lee Board' on pages 19 to 21 to learn more.

Kiln Posts: (aka, risers) Mullite clay posts are available in an assortment of heights. Posts are used to raise kiln shelves off the kiln floor plus they are used to support and raise molds when deep slumping (see page 46) or dropout forming (see page 49). Sometimes fusers will improvise other materials into service as risers, such as fiberboard strips or firebrick slices.

Glass Forming Mold Types

Molds are an essential component when kiln forming glass. A mold can be made from nearly any material that can withstand the temperature required for 3 dimensional glass forming.

Types of shaping that require molds:

• **Draping**: forming over a mold (see ProTip at left)

• **Slumping**: forming into a mold (see ProTip at left)

• **Dropout: (or deep-drop)** gravity dropping the glass down and through a mold (see page 49). Dropout and deep-drop molds are usually flat forms with an opening in the center. They are raised off the kiln floor using kiln posts to allow the glass to 'drop' down through the opening stretching toward the kiln shelf. The glass may be stopped before it hits the shelf (as we did in the Lazy Vase Project page 46) or it may be allowed to come to rest and flatten out on the kiln shelf (covered with release) a few inches below (as we did for the fountain basin on page 51).

• **Casting**: Uses a mold referred to as a 'dam' to confine and shape glass that has been heated to a near molten state (as we did in the Wall Vase Project page 68). Casting dam's can be made from fiberboard, fiber paper, firebrick (lined with mold release material) clay and other materials.

Common Mold Materials

• **Alumina Silica 'Fiberboard'**: soft, porous, rigid board, easy to cut & shape, available in thicknesses of: 1", 1 1/2" & 2" (25, 38 & 50 mm). This product is gaining popularity among fusers as a versatile mold material. It can be cut, carved and shaped easily and makes superb slump & drape molds, casting dams as well as kiln shelves. This material offers many advantages over traditional clay and stainless steel molds due to the unique characteristics of nominal expansion and extremely low heat absorption and heat retention. For more details be sure to read 'Working with KL board' on pages 19 to 20.

• **Casting Cement: (Refractory Cement)** for custom shapes. There are several castable products available that enable fusers to create a custom shaped mold by casting into or over a pre-formed model or by hand forming. Refractory cement is specially formulated to trap microscopic air pockets in the mix that provide a high degree of insulation. Casting cement in formulator expel the moisture content in the mix during curing to prevent steam flash off during the firing. Casting cement forms will last anywhere from 1 or 2 to several firings depending on brand specifications.

• **Clay: (Bisque Fired Ceramic)** in assorted shapes. Clay slumping molds are available in a great variety of shapes, sizes and uses, for plates, bowls, dishes, platters and more. It is necessary to pre-fuse a flat glass blank, then slump your glass blank into the mold for a second firing. Clay molds require a few small ventilation holes to allow the air to escape as the glass slumps into the mold; otherwise huge bubbles will deform the glass. If you have a new mold without holes, use a 1/8" (3 mm) carbide drill bit to make 3 to 5 strategically placed holes. Then make sure to keep the holes open after each application of kiln wash.

• **Fiber products:** This general category of products offer a very special quality for fusers - they do not stick to glass! These materials can be used to create an independent forming mold, they can modify the shape of another mold or they can be used as a primary or an auxiliary mold release (See next page for list).

Alumina silica (KL Board) fiberboard molds cut, carved and shaped, ready for kiln forming duty.

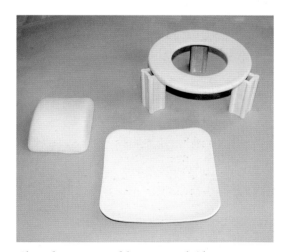

Clay slumping molds are available in a great variety of shapes, sizes and uses. Clockwise from top right, a drop out ring mold, a plate mold and a barrette mold.

ProTip

Clay Molds - Expansion And Contraction
Virtually all mold materials expand as they are heated and contract as they cool, as does glass. The problem is most expand and contract by varying amounts and at different temperatures. I will spare you the technical details and say that the differences between the expansion and contraction of glass and clay means that clay is great for slumping (into) but is not so good for draping (over). The simple explanation is glass can shrink tightly around the clay and lock itself onto the mold, usually cracking the glass in the process. If the drape is a loose 'free-form' style you will get away with it - never the less the 'rule of thumb' remains; slump into clay and drape over stainless steel, but you can slump into and drape over KL Board.

Heat Absorption And Retention For Molds

A successful fuse or form firing requires even and balanced heating and cooling of the glass. Since clay (and stainless steel) molds absorb and retain heat at completely different rates than the glass does, you must pay careful attention to the ramping up and cooling down speed of your firing schedule. It's imperative to heat and cool the work at a deliberate and consistent rate to prevent shocking the glass due to uneven heat distribution. In addition glass will stick to clay (and stainless steel), making the application of release a very important requirement (see release choices starting on page 17).

This casting dam was cut from a piece of 1/8" (3 mm) fiber paper - see project on page 82.

Refractory firebrick, a full size brick along with various cutoff pieces that are used for shelf and mold support.

An assortment of stainless steel drape molds coated with boron nitride resist.

- **Fiber Paper:** 1/32" & 1/8" (1 mm & 3 mm) thick, soft, flexible hi-temp material that can be used as a mold separator (see page 63) for a shallow dam mold (see page 82) or to kiln carve glass (see page 52).

- **Fiber Blanket**: 1/2" (1.5 cm) & 1" (2.5 cm) soft fluffy 'blanket-like', this hi-temp material has multiple uses in a fusing studio including the modification of an existing mold.

- **Fiber Blanket with rigidizer:** a flexible (moldable) sheet that can be creatively shaped then dried to form a hardened mold with a one of a kind shape (limit of 5 to 10 firings).

- **Fiberboard** - see Alumina Silica 'Fiberboard' at the top of page 15.

• **Firebrick: (Refractory)** for carving or damming. Firebrick has a variety of uses from kiln manufacturing to kiln furniture. It is very rigid but can be cut, carved and shaped using assorted woodworking tools. Firebrick is often used as a sturdy support to raise a shelf off the kiln floor (in place of kiln posts).

• **Natural Materials**: sand, stone. Only certain types of stone are able to withstand the high temperature required for glass forming, be sure to do test firings. One common use would be to creatively arrange a number of stones on a shelf and cover them with fiber paper. Then slump a glass blank over them to make an organic free form sculpture.

• **Stainless Steel: (formed sheet metal)** in assorted shapes. Stainless steel molds should only be used for draping due to the difference in expansion and contraction as compared to the glass. If you slump into a stainless steel mold, it will shrink faster than the glass as it cools and could lock tightly around the glass, causing it to break (see 'Clay Molds - Expansion And Contraction' on page 15 for more on this subject). Stainless steel molds are readily available in many shapes and from several sources. Your fused glass supplier will have several shapes made especially for glass draping - such as the wave shape we used for 'Project 9 - The Wave' on page 62. In addition, stainless steel containers made for kitchen & restaurant use can be effective molds. Items such as bowls, cups and trays, among other shapes can be used for draping. Be careful that the mold you use does not have an undercut or waistline. I remember an early experiment (a long time ago) when I stacked two floral formers (see ProTip on page 61) on top of each other in an attempt to fire a bigger floral shaped vase. However by doing that I created a waistline - a slightly narrowed area where the upper cup sits on the lower cup. When the glass slumped it clenched into that waistline, preventing me from removing the upper stainless steel cup. We had to physically cut the cup out using metal shears to rescue the glass vase. I didn't make that mistake again!

A Final Word About Molds

It is safe to say that the majority of fusing artists use clay molds as their primary choice for kiln forming. There are literally hundreds of models to choose from and you will find them in virtually every art glass supply store. Clay molds have been in use from the beginning of the glass fusing movement and they've earned their place on the fusing tool shelf.

However I rarely use clay molds in my work. My interest and strength as a glass artist is not so much about color embellishment and ornamentation. I tend to focus more on down-to-earth form, minimal color and multifaceted structure. Some people consider my artistic style to be minimalist or purist. However, minimalist and purist art should not be boring and that is my challenge - to add enough interest to please my own taste and hopefully to charm others as well. I rely more on shape rather than decoration for my work. That is why I'm drawn to the versatility and freedom of working with fiber products over clay molds. I appreciate the work of glass artists who concentrate on detailed surface work and I understand why they tend to choose straightforward classic shapes that are offered by the many traditional clay mold selections.

Resist, Release, Kiln Wash - Three Words One Effect!

Kiln wash is often referred to as the traditional release because for many years it was the only choice available. Mix 1 part kiln wash powder with 4 parts water, then paint it on your shelf or mold as evenly as you can, applying 3 to 4 coats. Then patiently wait until it totally dries (which takes about 2 to 3 days here in humid Florida).

Then there is the question of how many times you can fire on a kiln washed shelf. Some fusers will get several firings, while others recommend scraping the kiln wash off the shelf after each firing and reapply it. Besides being a lot of work, kiln wash isn't a totally reliable resist. Depending on the glass used and the ultimate temperature of the firing, kiln wash particles can stick to the glass and can be difficult, if not impossible to remove. Fusers have learned a lot more about releases and today we have several choices available.

Kiln Wash: there are several brands of high fire kiln wash available, all of them create a solid ceramic-like surface on the mold or kiln shelf. They will need to be removed after one or perhaps a few firings, depending on the product and temperature of the firing. When the kiln wash begins to loosen in some areas, it is time to remove it and re-wash. Note: KL board is the exception, you do not need to remove kiln wash from KL board, just apply it.

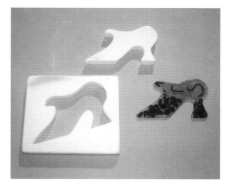

A KL board cutout mold that can be used as a drape mold (top), a slump mold (left) or use it for frit casting - as we did when we made this stylized high heel shoe (at right).

This multi-stage fiberboard mold can be used for shallow plates or deep bowls - see photos on page 20 for more details.

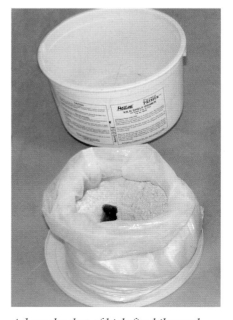

A large bucket of high fire kiln wash.

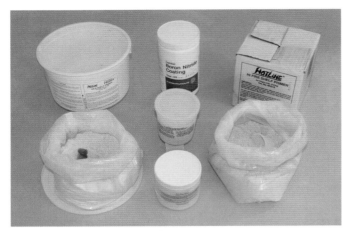

Primo Primer: a special kind of kiln wash that turns to dust after every firing. Requires a 500°F (260°C) cure-firing first to prevent it from sticking to the glass. Extremely easy to remove but must be reapplied (and cure-fired) before each use.

Boron Nitride: liquid form, most commonly used for stainless steel molds because it sticks to steel better than kiln wash. Since stainless steel molds are used only for draping at approximately 1200°F (649°C), the boron will stay on for many firings.

Thinfire™ paper: also called "thin release paper" comes on a roll or cut into sheets, this release turns to dust after a single firing. This is currently our favorite release since there is no prep time, the bottom surface of the glass is relatively smooth and it never sticks to the glass at any temperature. In addition we have discovered a method of pre fire assembly that entails gluing the glass pieces to the paper, making an easier build and less risky transport to the kiln.

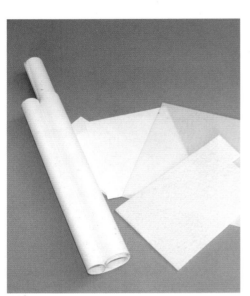

Fiber Paper: (See listing on page 16) can be used as a shelf release in a full-fuse firing but it will increase the occurrence of edge spikes - due to the way the glass forms to the soft surface. When fiber paper is used as a mold release in a slump or drape firing (as we did in the wave project on page 63) the temperature is low enough that spikes will not form. Try sifting a little dry kiln wash powder on the surface of the fiber paper to reduce the formation of spikes and to allow the glass to lift off the paper with less disruption and you will get a few additional firings out of the piece of fiber paper.

Release for Fiberboard Kiln Shelves and Molds

As I have stated many times already in this book, (and will no doubt say it again) I prefer to use Alumina Silica 'Fiberboard - specifically KL board - for my kiln shelves and forming molds. Fiberboard provides 4 additional release options.

1. No Kiln Wash - the surface of an uncoated fiberboard is course and the bottom surface of the glass will be rough and some of the fiberboard particles may stick temporarily to the glass (it comes off easily). I usually do not like this surface texture, except when I'm making tiles, as the rough surface improves the grip when installing.

2. Iridescent Side Down - The iridescent coating on glass functions as its own release and does not stick to fiberboard. This also works to increase the release on other materials as well. In addition the fiber particles actually intensify the iridescent look (this is also true when using fiber paper).

3. Kiln Wash Powder - I keep a nylon 'knee-high' sock filled with dry kiln wash powder with my release supplies and I use it to 'sift' powder on my fiberboard and fiber paper molds. This enhances the release effect on previous kiln washed fiber molds and increases the number of firings I can get out of a fiber paper release before it disintegrates.

4. Mica Powder - This product is available in assorted colors and is normally used to create surface decoration effects. However Patty Gray (a fusing celebrity) gave me a wonderful hint, spread mica powder on the uncoated surface of fiberboard and rub it into the porous surface. It will prevent sticking, make the glass surface smooth and gives the surface a nice shine.

Kaiser Lee Board

What is Kaiser Lee Board?

Alumina Silica 'Fiberboard' is a rigid but lightweight material that does not absorb or retain heat, helping to ensure a balanced heat distribution to the glass. For this reason fiberboard makes superb kiln shelves and fusing platforms, slump & drape molds, casting dams and more. This 'balanced heating' is an extremely important aspect that I will explain in greater detail in 'The Secret To Successful Firing' presented below. A few major brands of fiberboard available in the glass fusing market are Kaiser Lee Board, Duraboard™ and Fiberfrax™.

Are There Differences?

The answer is yes, but that needs some explanation. The 'Kaiser' part in 'Kaiser Lee Board' is not a coincidence. My husband Wolfgang and I own the company that repurposed this innovative product for the fusing industry. There are other alumina silica boards on the market but these have some drawbacks. If you are thinking we are biased in favor of our own board, you would be correct. However we have some very good reasons why we decided to put our name on this product.

The most noticeable feature that sets Kaiser Lee Board apart is that it is ready to use right out of the box. Other fiberboard brands require pre-use preparation steps such as a 'burnout' firing to release the organic binders. After burnout these other fiberboards are extremely soft and must be coated with a rigidizer to harden, then dry before use. The advantage of KL board is that it is finished under controlled conditions at the factory to ensure quality. As you might expect this feature means that it is more expensive, but KL board lasts for years when handled and stored correctly.

The Secret To Successful Firing

Whether fusing or forming glass, the key to success is even and balanced heating and cooling of the glass. This is a generalization, but the point is glass reacts adversely to inconsistent heat. We know that glass shrinks as it cools. When the top surface of the glass cools quicker than the bottom surface, the top surface also shrinks faster than the bottom surface. If the heating or cool down is too rapid (i.e. if the kiln was opened during cool down), the glass will be stressed and will most likely fracture.

In an ideal firing the entire mass of the glass (top, center and bottom) would be exactly the same temperature throughout the entire heating and cooling cycle. The problem is glass has to rest on something and if it is placed on a clay shelf (or mold) the bottom surface of the glass will heat up at the same rate as the shelf (or mold) while the top surface of the glass would heat up at a different rate, since it is not influenced by the heating of the shelf. The solution is to heat the kiln slow enough to allow the glass temperature to keep pace with the shelf (or mold) temperature.

A stainless steel putty knife is a great tool for cutting KL board. Press the knife gently into the board a small amount all the way around, empty dust by turning the KL board over, then keep going a few more millimeters at a time until you are all the way through. Cutting in one movement will break away the backside.

An effective way to create a KL board frit casting mold is to carve it using a round tipped blade in a craft knife.

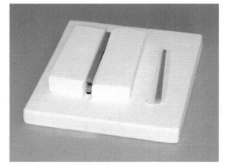

A simple dam set up used to create a small stacked square rod. I often fabricate small components like these to fill any empty space I might have in my large kiln when I'm firing a project. Otherwise the space is waisted and I lose an opportunity to make some interesting material for future projects.

Modify the shape of a KL board mold by placing board cutout forms in the corners (top & bottom right) along the sides (top left) or scatter broken chunks around the perimeter (bottom left) to add texture to the border of a slumped object.

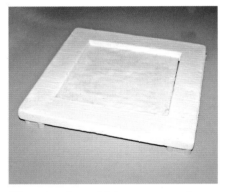

This simple mold is set up to slump a plate with a very shallow drop by leaving the center cutout in the hole and lifting the outer frame by only 1/4" (6 mm).

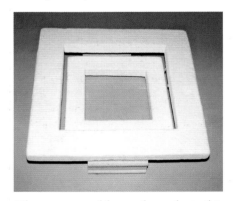

The same mold as above but this one is set up to create a two-stage drop bowl. The center would be 3" (7.6 cm) deep and the 2nd stage rim would be 2" (5 cm) deep.

The same is true for the cool down. The clay shelf (or mold) will retain heat longer than the glass due to the shelf's (or mold's) physical makeup. The bottom of the glass surface will always be hotter than the top surface of the glass due to the radiant heat from the clay shelf. That is why we have you adjust your anneal soak time, to wait for the clay shelf to reach 960°F (515°C).

There is another, even better solution, KL fiberboard! It is rigid enough to be used as a kiln shelf, yet soft enough to be carved into hundreds of different mold shapes and the best part is it does not conduct or retain heat. When glass is fired on this fiberboard the bottom surface will have the same temperature as the top surface because the shelf does not absorb or radiate heat. Virtually everything I build in my kiln uses KL board in one way or another and I have to say without question that KL board is the secret to the success and versatility of my projects. As you might expect, the other fiberboard products on the market can be successfully utilized for the projects in the book, provided that you follow the manufacturers directions for pre-use preparation.

A Teachers Duty

Ever since my students asked me, "Why in the world are you teaching us the 'old' way when you know an easier, more versatile and successful way?" (see more on this story in my 'Author Message' on page 4) I realized that my duty as a teacher was to show my students the easiest most reliable and most dependable way I know to kilnwork glass.

So What Can You Make With It?

After 8 years of experimenting with KL board I continue to discover new possibilities for it. For example, make a simple mold by cutting an 8" (20 cm) square from the center of a 12" (30 cm) piece of KL board (see center cut molds in photos at left). Then use that same mold for all of the following possibilities:

1. Slump a plate with a very shallow drop by leaving the center cutout in the hole and lifting the outer frame 1/4" (6 mm) (photo left center)

2. Slump a shallow bowl (a 1" drop) by removing the center cutout and setting the mold directly on the kiln shelf. (not shown)

3. Modify the shape of the dropout by placing fiberboard cutout forms in the corners (photo upper left)

4. Modify the center of the mold by placing a fiberboard strip across the space to divide the slump bowl into 2 reservoirs

4. Slump a deeper bowl by placing the mold on 1" (2.5 cm) risers to create a 2" (5 cm) bowl drop

5. Deep slump a vase by setting the mold on 4" to 6" (10 to 15 cm) risers, either stop the drop before it hits the kiln shelf (see Lazy Vase on page 46) or allow the drop to hit the shelf to create a flat-base bottom

6. Use the mold as a casting dam to make a square cast glass sculpture (see Wall Vase page 68)

7. Modify the casting dam by placing fiberboard cutout forms inside the square (see Wall Vase page 68)

8. Rake the surface of the sculpture to create swirls, the casting dam will maintain the shape (see Rake It page 72)

There Must Be A Catch!

Kaiser Lee Board does cost more than the other fiberboards on the market. Some perceive it as expensive and for a time I believed that as well. But after years of experience and positive feedback from so many glass artists, I now know the opposite is true. I am often asked, "How long will KL board last"? (or how many firings)? The answer is "way too long for our liking". Some of the KL board shelves that I have in my studio are over eight years old, they have been fired hundreds of times and are still going strong (our accountant would prefer the boards would self destruct after one year).

Seriously the only drawback I can think of with KL board is that it is fairly easy to break or dent and of course you need to wear protection for the dust, which is true for all brands of fiberboard. Handle your shelves and molds carefully and store them in boxes when not in use. Always wear a dust mask when cutting or carving fiberboard to avoid breathing the dust. Work on a flat surface with several layers of newspapers, then discard one layer of the newspaper on a regular basis as the dust mounts up. Other than those few caveats - it's all good fun!

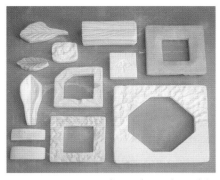

An assortment of KL board molds. We have used many of these molds several dozen times and they continue to work as if they were just made.

A basic 2 squares cutout mold that has been modified using a few simple building block shapes. We used a similar mold set up to cast the pen holders on page 74 bottom right.

The Essential Safety Lecture - *Don't Learn Safety by Accident!*

The most valuable piece of safety equipment in your studio is your brain! It's important to *think* your way through each activity. You can be dangerous and take risks with your designs but not when it comes to personal safety. Here's a few things for you to *think* about to enhance your fusing fun.

- We know raw cut glass is razor-sharp but if you *think* to put the sheets away the instant you're done with them you'll reduce glass cuts (and Band-Aid use) substantially.
- Kilns get hot… hot enough to melt glass (good thing to) so you have to *think* about keeping anything flammable (like your hands) away from hot kilns and you should also *think* about having one or two fire extinguishers nearby.
- *Think* about how wonderful eyesight is then *think* to wear safety glasses whenever you're cutting, shaping, grinding, drilling, or manipulating materials in any manner.
- Whenever you're working with powdered materials, *think* to wear a respirator. Protect your lungs from, kiln wash, mold release, fiberboard dust (when cutting or carving), thin release paper (after it's fired), fiber paper, glass frit powders, etc.
- *Think* about keeping your studio neat & tidy, have good lighting and clever storage (& use it), close chemical containers immediately, sweep your workbench regularly and don't eat dichroic glass (even though I know you're tempted).
- Keep a watchful eye on curious studio guests, everything looks appealing and cool - they don't know the dangers that may lurk nearby, so you have to *think* for them.

Finally *think* about how much fun fusing is, let yourself play like a child in the fields of colorful glass but *think* what could happen if you didn't stop to *think* - and something happened.

Firing Schedules

You will find every firing schedule that you'll need for the projects in this book on the following page. These 8 schedules encompass 90% of the firings that fusers perform on a regular basis. They have rather generic titles that describe the type of firing they were designed for but what if your piece doesn't fit into one of these descriptions? The answer is... design your own!

Design Your Own Firing Schedule - It's Easy!

All you have to do is assess your project, the desired size and thickness, decide which process you want to achieve, then choose the key target temperatures and times. That's all there is to it! You will have a custom schedule created specifically for your work.

1st Consideration - Ramping Up

This is the initial heating phase of any firing, from room temperature to 1000°F (535°C). Heating too quickly through this range could seriously stress the glass causing it to shatter from thermal shock. Careful matching of the 'ramp up' speed to the body-mass (the size & thickness) of the glass will eliminate the stress.

'Ramp Up' for First Firing

First firing refers to the first time a work is fired after the pre-fuse assembly. The ramp up speed should be between 10°F & 20°F (4°C & 16°C) per minute (if you prefer degrees per hour see HotTip above). There would be no harm in ramping up every firing at the slowest ramp speed but in the interest of conserving electricity and time, I prefer to fine-tune the ramp speed based on the size of the largest piece of glass in my assembly. The following list assumes 2 layers of standard thickness glass or 1 base layer plus a decorative accent layer.

- All small pieces (e.g. jewelry) or casting with frit chunks - ramp up at 30°F (16°C) per minute.
- Under 1 sq/ft (900 sq/cm) - ramp up at 15°F (9°C) per minute.
- Between 1 sq/ft (900 sq/cm) & 1 1/2 sq/ft (1400 sq/cm) - ramp up at 12°F (7°C) per minute.

> **HotTip**
>
> Many of the fusing books, glass manufacturers and/or digital kiln controllers list ramp speeds in Degrees Per Hour (DPH). We prefer to use Degrees Per Minute (DPM) because that is what our digital controller requires but it's easy to convert from DPM to DPH. Simply multiply the DPM by 60 (the number of minutes in an hour) to get the degrees per hour (works for both °F or °C). For example 15 DPM would be 15 x 60 = 900 DPH. It's that simple!

- Over 1 1/2 sq/ft (1400 sq/cm) - ramp up at 10°F (6°C).
- The assembly is bigger or contains some decorative components that were previously fused - ramp up at 6°F (4°C) per minute.

'Ramp Up' for Previously Fused Work

When re-firing previously fused work the ramp up speed must be slowed down considerably. Remember you are now heating a thicker single piece of glass that will be much slower to absorb the heat. Whether you're fire polishing, draping, slumping or adding more design elements, use the mass of the glass to determine the ramp up speed. Some experienced fusers suggest a ramp speed that is half the speed they used for the first fuse firing. This may work but I hate to lose a piece at this stage of the game so I play it safe and ramp up most of my pre-fused work at 5°F (3°C) per minute.

Exception To The Rule: When fire polishing or re-firing a jewelry piece it's OK to ramp up a bit faster, at 10°F (6°C) per minute. A cast glass piece must ramp up slower, 3°F (1°C) per minute.

'Target Up Pre-Soak' (optional)

As an extra precaution, I've programmed my digital controller to hold for 10 minutes once the ramp up phase has reached 1000°F (538°C) to make sure the glass is fully heated and stabilized before proceeding to the 'Target Up' phase.

Schedule A - Small Pieces - 1st Full Fuse

Phase	Deg Per Min	Target Temp	Action
Ramp Up	30°F / 16°C	1000°F / 538°C	Soak 1 min
Target Up	Full-speed	1470°F / 799°C	Hold 10 min
Anneal Soak	Hold	960°F / 516°C	10 min
Anneal Cool	---	Room	---
Turn off & cool down to room temperature - Do Not Peek			

Schedule B - Medium - 1st Full Fuse

Phase	Deg Per Min	Target Temp	Action
Ramp Up	15°F / 9°C	1000°F / 538°C	Soak 10 min
Target Up	Full-speed	1450°F / 788°C	Hold 12+ min
Anneal Soak	Hold	960°F / 516°C	60 min
Anneal Cool	5°F / 3°C	700°F / 371°C	5 min
Turn off & cool down to room temperature - Do Not Peek			

Schedule C - Large - 1st Full Fuse

Phase	Deg Per Min	Target Temp	Action
Ramp Up	12°F / 7°C	1000°F / 538°C	Soak 10 min
Target Up	Full-speed	1440°F / 782°C	Hold 15+ min
Anneal Soak	Hold	960°F / 516°C	90 min
Anneal Cool	5°F / 3°C	700°F / 371°C	10 min
Turn off & cool down to room temperature - Do Not Peek			

Schedule D - Extra Large - 1st Full Fuse

Phase	Deg Per Min	Target Temp	Action
Ramp Up	10°F / 6°C	1000°F / 538°C	Soak 1 min
Target Up	Full-speed	1430°F / 777°C	Hold 18+ min
Anneal Soak	Hold	960°F / 516°C	120 min
Anneal Cool	5°F / 3°C	700°F / 371°C	15 min
Turn off & cool down to room temperature - Do Not Peek			

Schedule E - Medium/Large - Drape

Phase	Deg Per Min	Target Temp	Action
Ramp Up	5°F / 3°C	1000°F / 538°C	Soak 10 min
Target Up	Full-speed	1210°F / 655°C	Hold 5+ min
Anneal Soak	Hold	960°F / 516°C	60 to 90 min
Anneal Cool	5°F / 3°C	700°F / 371°C	5 min
Turn off & cool down to room temperature - Do Not Peek			

Schedule F - Medium/Large - Slump

Phase	Deg Per Min	Target Temp	Action
Ramp Up	5°F / 3°C	1000°F / 538°C	Soak 10 min
Target Up	Full-speed	1280°F / 695°C	Hold 10+ min
Anneal Soak	Hold	960°F / 516°C	90 min
Anneal Cool	5°F / 3°C	700°F / 371°C	10 min
Turn off & cool down to room temperature - Do Not Peek			

Schedule G - Medium/Large - Deep Drop

Phase	Deg Per Min	Target Temp	Action
Ramp Up	5°F / 3°C	1000°F / 538°C	Soak 10 min
Target Up	Full-speed	1265°F / 685°C	Hold 45+ min
Anneal Soak	Hold	960°F / 516°C	90 min
Anneal Cool	5°F / 3°C	700°F / 371°C	5 min
Turn off & cool down to room temperature - Do Not Peek			

Schedule H - Frit Casting

Phase	Deg Per Min	Target Temp	Action
Ramp Up	30°F / 16°C	1000°F / 538°C	Soak 15 min
Target Up	Full-speed	1470°F / 799°C	Hold 12+ min
Anneal Soak	Hold	960°F / 516°C	120 min
Anneal Cool	4°F / 2°C	700°F / 371°C	25 min
Turn off & cool down to room temperature - Do Not Peek			

Venting Through Ramp Up (optional)

We no longer recommend venting during ramp up. The original purpose of venting was to release the burn-off vapors and residues from materials like assembly glue, shelf release, or mold binders. The new and improved glue and release materials do not require venting and since our shelves and molds are made from KL board (that is pre-fired in the factory) we do not encounter burn-off. However if you suspect some items in your firing could produce burn off residues, you should vent. Block the lid open about 1/2" (1.5 cm) and do not remove the vent until the kiln reaches 1000°F (535°C), then close the lid, perform a 'Target Up Pre-Soak' to ensure the heat is properly balanced.

2nd Consideration - 'Target Up' Phase

The 'Target Up' phase (aka Rapid Heat) will push the kiln rapidly up to the 'Target Arrival Temperature.' The glass is well past the critical stage and you can safely raise the temperature as fast as your kiln will go.

'Bubble Squeeze' Soak (optional)

Air bubbles can form between stacked layers, especially between layers of smooth glass, the larger the pieces the more likely bubbles will form. If you think your assembly may be susceptible you should execute

Process	Target Arrival Temperature
Draping	1150°F to 1250°F 620°C to 675°C
Slumping	1250°F to 1380°F 675°C to 745°C
Fire polishing	1300°F to 1400°F 705°C to 760°C
Tack fusing	1320°F to 1400°F 730°C to 790°C
Full fusing	1400°F to 1550°F 790°C to 845°C
Frit casting	1480°F to 1600°F 805°C to 870°C
Pate de Verré	1400°F to 1600°F 815°C to 870°C
Raking / Combing	1650°F to 1750°F 900°C to 955°C
Full-melt Casting	1700°F to 1800°F 925°C to 980°C
Crucible (Pot) Melt	1700°F to 2000°F 927°C to 1093°C

ProTip
Devitrification
Glass can devitrify (a hazy surface crystallization) if it's held for an extended period between 1330°F & 1400°F (720°C & 760°C). The objective is to move the glass through this range as swiftly as possible (both up and down). Most 'fusible' glass made today has been formulated to reduce the occurrence of devitrification. It is still a good idea to move through the 'devit-zone' quickly but it's not as critical as it once was.

a 'bubble squeeze' soak. Set the controller to soak for 10 to 15 minutes at 1225°F (663°C). The objective is to slow down the draping rate of the top layer, to allow time for the air to escape before the layers fuse and trap the bubbles inside.

3rd Consideration - 'Target Arrival Temp'

This is the temperature required to accomplish the intended process of your work (forming, fusing, casting, etc). The chart on this page lists the most common kiln working processes along with a 'Target Arrival' temperature range. We've used a range to make an allowance for the inconsistency between pyrometers, kiln speeds and the duration of the target soak. Notice the "full fusing" target temperature is between 1400°F & 1550°F (790°C & 845°C). A successful firing involves more than simply reaching a specific target temperature, it also requires a soak period to allow time for the effect to occur. It is usually best to choose a target temperature from low to middle of the target range then soak at that temperature for a longer time. For instance a full fuse firing with a target temperature of 1490°F (810°C), held for 10 minutes should produce a similar result as a lower target temperature of 1450°F (788°C) held for 15 minutes. The advantage at the lower end is the process happens slower, giving you more time to observe and react to better control the outcome (you can always push the temperature a bit during the firing if needed). Remember these temperatures may not be correct for your kiln. Be sure to monitor your own firings until you have determined the best target temperature and hold times for the kiln and type of firings that you are doing.

4th Consideration - 'Temperature down'

As soon as you are confidant that the glass has reached the final appearance you are striving for, (confirmed by a visual inspection) simply turn the kiln down (better yet, set the controller) to allow the kiln to cool naturally to the anneal soak temperature of 960°F (516°C). It is not necessary to flash cool (open the door) to bring the temperature down quickly. We don't usually flash cool, except for drape or drop out firings where we open the kiln to observe the glass at the target temperature. We usually load our kiln, set the controller to run the required schedule and forget it until morning.

5th Consideration - 'Anneal Soak'

The anneal soak phase is important to stabilize and remove internal stress in the glass. Proper annealing involves two factors, the soak temperature and the soak time period. The anneal soak temperature is given to us by the glass manufacturers. The average for fusing glass is 960°F (516°C) (for a more specific anneal temperature check the glass manufacturers website for the glass you are using).

The optimum soak time is a bit more difficult to determine. The main factor is the body-mass of the glass. The larger the body-mass (thicker glass &/or larger piece) the longer it must be soaked at the annealing temperature. My rule of thumb for anneal soak times is as follows:

- Smaller pieces (like jewelry) - I turn off the kiln and let it cool down on its own.

- Small to medium size pieces, up to 2 layers thick - soak for 45 minutes

- Medium to larger pieces, 2 to 3 layers thick - soak for 60 minutes

- Large pieces, 3 or more layers over 1 sq/ft (900 sq/ cm) or cast pieces of any size up to 1/2" (1.3 cm) thick - soak for 120 to 180 minutes

If you're not sure which category your piece fits into, choose the longer soak time, an extra soak will not hurt your piece. Also if the kiln has more than one item in the load, be sure to choose the soak time for the largest piece (the smaller ones will be fine). If you want to do really big and thick pieces (e.g. sinks)

ProTip

You open your kiln after a firing and to your dismay, your work is lying there hopelessly broken into a dozen pieces. Once you get over the shock you need to figure out if the fracture happened during the temp up, or temp down phase. Examine one of the cracked pieces. Are all the edges rounded off or are they raw and sharp? Rounded edges indicate the break happened during the ramp up stage; sharp edges means it happened during cool down. Use this information to moderate the target up ramp speed or the anneal soak & cool timing on your next firing.

you'll need some expert advice, take a class or ask a glass manufacturer for more information.

6th Consideration - 'Anneal Cool'

When firing large pieces, 3 layers over 1 sq/ft (900 sq/cm) or cast pieces, it is good practice to slow the ramp down cooling from the 960°F (516°C) anneal soak to 700°F (371°C) This range the upper and lower end of the strain point. We program our kilns to anneal cool at a rate of 5°F (3°C) per minute.

7th Consideration - 'Final Cool'

This is the easiest step of all. Simply turn off the kiln and let it cool down to room temperature without opening the lid/door. This could take anywhere from 3 to 8 hours depending on the size and insulating qualities of the kiln. The main thing is - Don't Peek! (Nobody said this part would be easy!)

A Jewelry Ensemble

OK I'll admit it, when I go out I'm usually wearing one of my jewelry creations. In fact many people think the only items I make are jewelry. When they ask me "What the heck is glass fusing?" the first item I can usually show them is whatever piece (or pieces) of jewelry I happen to be wearing. In addition - Jewelry sells! A good number of my students support themselves (or at least support their fusing habit) by creating and selling fused jewelry. You will find plenty of good books on the subject of fused glass jewelry. In fact my publisher has some excellent books on this theme (see the book flyer on last page in this book). For this reason I will limit the jewelry projects offered in this book to only these few - even though I have plenty of ideas for more. I have cleverly integrated a number of interesting techniques within these Jewelry Ensemble pieces, to enlighten and inspire your own creative jewelry designs.

Observations & Lessons

- Create an innovative expandable ring
- Embed fine silver hooks and bails as inclusions into your fused pieces
- Minimize discoloration of the silver and glass during firing
- Put a professional polish on the precious metal
- Embed cubic zirconium faceted stones as inclusions during fuse firing

Additional Items

Jeweler's Tools:
- Flush cutters (wire cutters), needle nosed pliers and flat pliers
- Jewelers hammer and anvil, wire brush and polishing paper
- Lapidary tumbler with stainless steel shot

Jewelry Supplies:
- Fine silver (.999) round wire - 18, 20 & 21 gauge
- Fine silver (.999) Cloisonne strip - 28 gauge, 3/16" (5 mm) wide
- Cubic zirconium (faceted stones), assorted shapes - 5 mm
- Glass seed beads - approximate size 1/8" (3 mm)
- Jewelers elastic cord (thread) - 1/32" (1 mm) diameter

Jewelry Ensemble Part 1 - Rings

When you are making a variety of rings to sell, you will often find that you have nearly every size - except the very size the customer standing in front of you needs (that may be one of Murphy's Laws for jewelers). Adjustable rings would seem to be the answer unfortunately they are not as highly valued by many buyers. My solution is to mount the fused stone along with some seed beads on an elastic cord (or thread) that is made especially for jewelry applications. Rather than call this ring style 'adjustable' I like to call it 'expandable'. I presented one of these expandable rings to my grandmother and to my surprise she mentioned a benefit that I had not even considered. She told me her problem with rings is her fingers swell up during the day and fixed size rings become very uncomfortable. "This ring" she declared, "is comfortable to wear all day!"

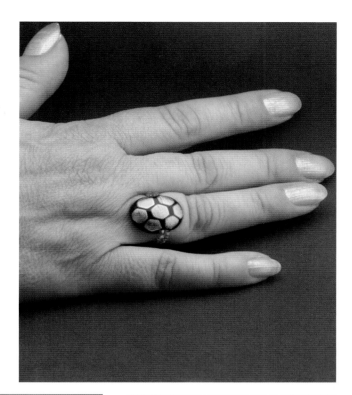

Expandable Ring

1. Choose and cut the glass piece that will be the top design of your ring. I used a honeycomb patterned dichroic glass and cut it to resemble a 6 petal flower. Use this top piece as a pattern to cut the base piece, I used thin black glass. You will also need 2 tiny pieces of the base glass, about 1/8" (3 mm) square (the shape is not critical). These will be used to level and balance the top piece leaving a space to place the fiber paper. Of course you could decorate the top using any variety of small pieces that your artistic heart desires.

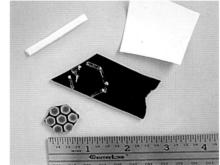

2. Clean your prepared glass pieces thoroughly. Pre-fired assemblies are easy to shift or knock over completely on the way to the kiln. That is why we recommend a little glue to keep everything in line. We like Glasstac™ glue, Hotline Fusers Glue, Thompson Klyr Fire™, or use a little white glue (children's glue is easy to mix and dries fast) thinned down with water, and a small artists paintbrush to apply it.

3. Cut a piece of thin release paper just large enough for the jewelry you will be firing. If you have some scrap shelf release this is a great time to use it up. Place it on your kiln shelf and glue your jewelry assemblies together, starting with gluing the base glass piece directly to the shelf release paper, a small dab of glue only please.

4. Continue to build up your pieces. Remember to add a thin piece of fiber paper across the middle of the bottom piece to create the through-hole for the elastic cord (glue it down as well). Glue the 1/8" (3 mm) square leveling pieces to either side of the fiber paper. These balance pieces will make easy work out of adding the top design piece.

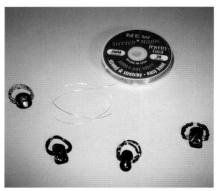

5. Load the kiln (adding other jewelry pieces for economy) and fire using: **Schedule A - Small Pieces - Full Fuse**, on page 23.

ProTip

The Reef Knot or Square Knot is known by anyone who was ever in Cub Scouts, Girl Guides, a boating club or had any outdoors training. The way to remember it is 'Right over left, and under, then left over right, and under. Pull to tighten. It really is that easy and it produces a very tight knot that is flatter and stronger than the old standby double knot (aka Granny Knot). Follow the illustrations here.

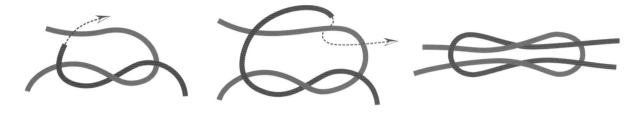

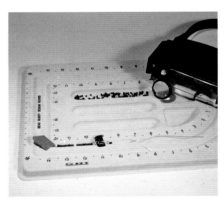

This bead assembly tray makes easy work of arranging and threading beads.

6. Remove the fiber paper by poking it through the cabochon with a long needle (or a piece of stiff wire). Cut a piece of the elastic cord about 10" (25 cm) long and secure one end to the bead assembly tray with a piece of masking tape. Then string some seed beads until you have enough to go around a finger once, about 2" (5 cm). Now thread your fused cabochon onto the string and finish with another 2" (5 cm) of seed beads on the other side of the cabochon.

7. The last step is to push the loose end of the elastic cord through the cabochon once more. Then remove the tape on the other end and tie the cord together with a reef knot (aka 'square knot') see ProTip above.

8. The finishing touch is to secure the knot with a drop of clear nail polish then slide the beads on the cord until the knot is hidden inside the cabochon.

Spiral Wrapped Ring

Chole, one of my students inspired this design when she was not thrilled with the pendant she had made. She decided to take the pendant to her personal jeweler to have a ring made using a sterling silver wire wrapping technique. This is a variation on that theme.

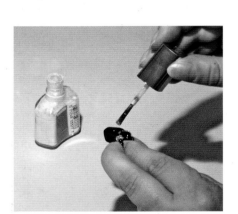

1. Create a 'finger sized' form using a piece of KL board (similar to a jewelers ring mandrel). Wrap the form with a small piece of thin release paper and secured it with a dab of glue.

2. Next wrap two revolutions of 16 gauge fine silver wire around a jewelers ring mandrel near the size that you want the ring to be (the exact size is not critical since the ring is expandable).

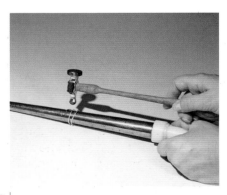

3. Slide the wire off the mandrel and onto the KL board 'finger' form. Then set up 2 scrap pieces of KL board in the kiln and carefully balance the finger form across them.

4. Finally cut and place a piece of black glass under each end of the wire and another one on top (I used a pieces of dichroic). You have to carefully balance and level the two level pieces of thin black glass on the finger form making sure the wire is sandwiched between them on both ends. I know glue seems like a good idea, unfortunately glue will only hold until it burns off then if the top glass is not balanced it could slide off and ruin the project.

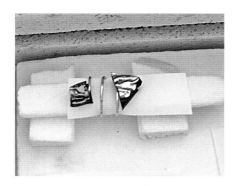

5. Load the kiln (adding other jewelry pieces if desired) and fire using: **Schedule A - Small Pieces - 1st Full Fuse**, on page 23.

Jewelry Ensemble Part 2
Pendant with Fine Silver & Cubic Zirconium

One of the many special benefits of teaching is that I often get as much out of a class as my students do. I always feel recharged from the energy and excitement that new students bring to the class and sometimes I acquire an actual 'gem' of a technique. That is exactly what happened when a student in our Las Vegas seminar wore a wonderful pendant to class that had 3 cubic zirconium 'gems' embedded directly into it. For this I have to send a thank you to that student for kindly sharing her technique of combining glass and cubic zirconium.

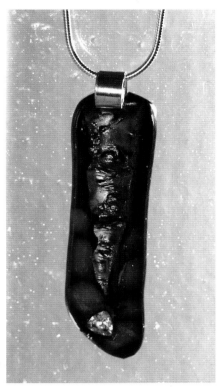

1. The idea is to embed the cubic zirconium directly into the glass so both the top and bottom of the CZ is exposed through the glass. This will allow light to strike the CZ from the back of the pendent and make it sparkle when viewed from the front. This process works best if the pendent is only a single layer of glass, at least at the spot where the CZ is going to be placed. The first thing to do is to decide on the size and shape of your pendent. I'm going to make mine a rectangle about 3/4" x 2 1/4" (2 x 6 cm). Of course you can make yours any size and shape that you desire.

2. The next step is to drill a hole where you plan to mount the CZ (or CZ's, place as many as you like). Use your high-speed portable drill (minimum 20,000 rpm) fitted with a 1/8" (3 mm) hollow-core diamond-coated drill bit (see ProTip at right).

3. Fill each drill hole with a tiny piece of used fiber paper, leaving just enough room for the pointy end of the CZ to sit down into the hole. The fiber paper will keep the hole open beneath the CZ. Without it the glass would close and there will be no light behind the stone.

 ProTip

Drilling Holes in Glass

• Always wear eye protection when drilling or grinding
• Check the tip of your hollow-core drill bit to make sure there is no glass left in there from the last use (if there is, knock it out) - see pro tip page 66.
• Always drill at the highest speed available on your rotary 'drill' tool.
• Keep your work lubricated and cool by drilling inside a shallow plastic tray with a piece of 1/8" (3 mm) standard clear window glass on the bottom and about 3/8" (1 cm) of water (just enough to cover your glass)
• Start by holding the drill at an angle (about 30° from perpendicular) until you have established a pilot spot, then move the drill to perpendicular (straight up) and do not push down too much. Patiently let the drill bit grind away until it is all the way through.

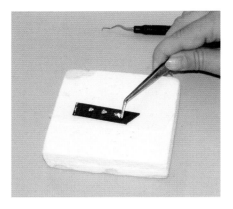

Fine Silver Loop Bail

4. Since this is a rather small, single layer pendant I think a fine silver bail will work best. I'm going to make a spiral bail from a 2" (5 cm) long piece of fine silver cloisonne strip 28 gauge, 3/16" (5 mm) wide. I put one end into the tip of my needle nose pliers and started winding it up leaving about 1/4" (6 mm) sticking out, or you could fashion a bail from round fine silver wire make a simple loop, or one with a spiral at both ends, any number of shapes would work - this is where you should unleash your creative playfulness to make something truly unique!

5. The last piece of glass that we need to cut is something to secure the bail during fusing. I selected a scrap piece of dichroic and shaped it into a long triangle to add a bit of décor to my pendant.

6. The final step is to assemble the whole thing. Start with a piece of thin release paper. Place the base glass on it and position the CZ in the hole (make sure the fiber paper is still in there). Place the bail at the top of the pendant (spiral up) then put a small pillow of fiber paper under the bail to hold its head up and cover the tongue with the dichroic glass. I scattered a few pieces of clear frit around the bottom section to provide some depth and volume.

7. That's all there is to it! Load the kiln and fire using: **Schedule A - Small Pieces - 1st Full Fuse**, on page 23.

ProTip

Adding silver to your fused projects is a fun and easy way to 'turn up the sizzle'. However, if you intend the silver to be an 'inclusion' (that is to be fused with the glass) by firing it in the kiln along with your glass you must use fine silver (.999) - not sterling silver. Sterling silver components will turn black and become brittle when exposed to the high fusing temperatures. You can use Sterling silver findings for final fabrication, such as earring loops, clasps, necklace chains, etc. so long as you are not firing the Sterling silver along with your glass.

Bonus

1: Fine silver reacts with some of our art glass - one common reaction is the fine silver discolors the glass - turning it black or white around the edge of your loop. This occurs more often with colored opalescent glass, and that is why we prefer to sandwich the silver between layers of black glass whenever possible. But other color combinations will work, so run some tests, keep careful notes and you will discover some exciting possibilities. Another discoloration concern is the silver turns gold under standard clear fusing glass. This can be avoided by using a specially formulated clear glass "called crystal clear" as the top cover.

2: Include 24 ct gold in your fused pieces in the same way you use pure silver; it is more expensive - but you're worth it!

3: Use the jewelers needle nose pliers and the flush cutters (wire cutters) to create a number of loops that can be embed into the glass (sandwiched between two layers) and use as the bail to hang the pendant from a chain. This same technique can be used for bracelets, earrings, pendants or any item that requires a bail loop to attach it to something else (see jewelry ensemble part 4 next page). You can also take the silver a step further using it as a major design element to offset your glass pieces. As always, the opportunities are endless.

Jewelry Ensemble Part 3 - Earrings with Fine Silver

1. The ability to embed fine silver directly into fused glass jewelry opens a world of design potential, especially for earrings, since they need to be as lightweight as possible. One of the easiest and most effective solutions is to create a small eye loop (shaped like a cotter pin, see photo at bottom right) and sandwich it between 2 layers of thin glass, the top layer usually has some design on, or added to it.

2. Load the kiln and fire it flat on a piece of thin release paper using: **Schedule A - Small Pieces - 1st Full Fuse**, on page 23.

3. Finish the earrings by hanging them on a French ear-wire with a few seed beads and instantly, you have created a lovely art piece. Add a lavish touch with a spiral made from 20 gauge fine silver round wire to extend the earring into a dangle style as we did in this photograph. So many possibilities!

Jewelry Ensemble Part 4
Cabochon Bracelet Using Fine Silver Wire

1. This project is simple and you can probably figure out how it's done just by looking at the photo. Basically I made a larger cabochon, about 1 1/2" (4 cm) square (the photo lower right gives some alternate cabochon shapes) and embedded 2 fine silver loops on either side. I used my round jaw pliers to form the eye-loops from 18 gauge fine silver round wire (the loops are approximately 1/4" (6 mm) in diameter). The tail end of the loops were sandwiched between the top and bottom layers of the glass components in the standard way and fired using: **Schedule B - Medium - 1st Full Fuse**, on page 23.

2. The silver bracelet shown in the photo at right is a standard, ready-made jewelry component available from most jewelry supply stores. Use the flat nosed pliers to flatten out the cabochon loops enough to allow the ends of the silver bracelet to fit inside. Pinch one end of the bracelet to close off the loop and leave the other end open just enough to allow the bracelet to be easily clipped on the wearer's wrist.

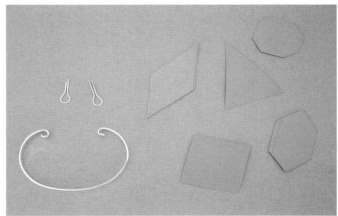

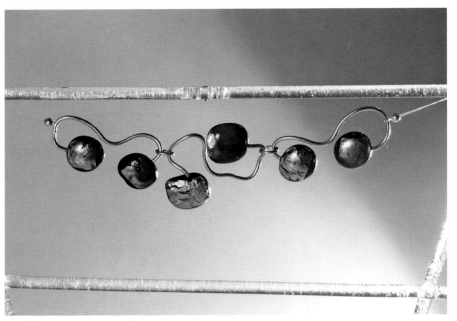

ProTip

Before you place your silver wire on the glass, hammer it carefully with the round tip of a jewelry hammer to leave a pattern. During firing your silver will get soft again, so you will be able to work-harden it by hammering it a second time. The reason for hammering it the first time is to get a consistent pattern on the silver. After firing it will be not possible to hammer the silver too close to the glass. This is also effective for the ring project.

Jewelry Ensemble Part 5 - Free-form Necklace Pendant

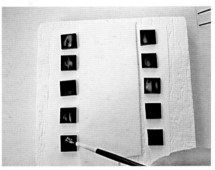

This necklace assembly is quite simple to make but has an impressive presentation. Even experienced fusers have to look closely to figure out how it's done.

1. Cut pieces of 16 gauge fine silver round wire, 3 1/2" (9 cm) long. Straighten them by rolling them back and forth on your bench under a wooden ruler.

2. Cut 1 piece of 1/8" (3 mm) thick fiber paper 2 1/2" x 6" (9 x 15 cm) and place the fiber paper on your kiln shelf. Cut 2 strips of thin release paper approximately 1" x 6" (2.5 x 15 cm) and lay the strips of thin release paper on either side of the fiber paper.

3. Arrange base pieces of glass, I made mine 1/2" (1 cm) square, on the thin release paper as shown in the photo above left. Place a dab of glue in the middle of each glass piece and lay the fine silver wires across from one glass to the other. The wire sits higher than the glass due to the thickness of the fiber paper we placed on the shelf.

4. Place and glue 2 small chips of base glass on either side of the wire on every piece. These chips will allow the top dichroic glass to balance across the wire. Finally place and glue the dichroic glass on top. Place the kiln shelf in your kiln and fire using: **Schedule A - Small Pieces - 1st Full Fuse**, on page 23.

5. Make the necklace shown in the top photo, by bending the wire into various shapes, then use 18 gauge oval jump rings, sterling or fine silver, to bind them together in a pleasing pattern. The necklace shown in the photo above uses 3 of these fused assemblies.

Jewelry Ensemble Part 6 - The Finishing Touch

A few years ago I was introduced to the 'lapidary tumbler.' This device has been around for a long time, however if you haven't seen the effect it has on silver and glass jewelry, then you're in for a pleasant surprise.

1. Simply fill the tumbler container 1/3 full with stainless steel shot (from a jewelry supply store) and 3/4 full with water and a drop of dishwashing soap.

2. Add a few jewelry pieces, 6 or so at a time, close the container tight and place it on the rotator. Turn the tumbler on and let it run for about 1 hour.

3. After tumbling, pour the stainless steel shot and the jewelry pieces through a kitchen strainer and rinse. Remove your jewelry pieces and let the shot dry before you put it back in storage (if you put it away wet it can tarnish). The stainless steel shot does not harm the glass but the silver on your jewelry gets really shiny and smooth. An additional advantage is that the relatively soft fine silver stiffness up from being 'work hardened.'

Bonus

I promised to give you a little something extra in this book - so here is a bonus silver & glass trick.

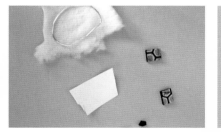

1: Cut 2 pieces of 20 gauge fine silver round wire 2 1/2" (6 cm) long. Bend each one into a circle and add a little texture by hammering them with the rounded end of your jewelers hammer.

2: Now place a piece of thin release paper on your kiln shelf and place an earring sized piece of black glass on it. Then lay the open part of the silver wire loop on the glass.

3: Place and glue the 1/8" (3 mm) square leveling glass pieces to either side of the wire. Then balance and glue the top design piece across the 2 leveling pieces.

4: Load the kiln and fire using: **Schedule A - Small Pieces - Full Fuse**, on page 23.

5: After firing you can shape the wire in any number of ways. I put a double oval shaped loop in mine and attached it to ear hooks. Use your imagination to take the glass and silver designing techniques to totally new artistic grounds.

6: Finish them in your lapidary tumbler to polish and work harden the fine silver.

Jewelry Display Stand

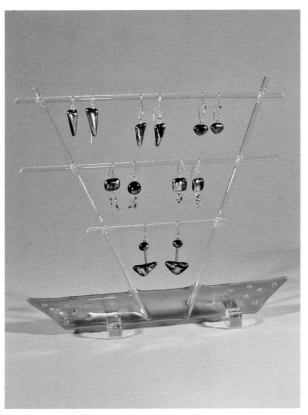

You can find a great variety of ready made displays for jewelry. At the lower end of the field are simple trays lined with black felt (either with or without glass lids) at the other end are some extensive pieces of furniture with glass doors, tops and halogen lights. Successful retail managers will tell you that a proper display for artwork and jewelry in particular is a key to sales success. Finding the perfect display for my glass jewelry has long been a challenge for me but I am very excited about this new sculptural way to show-off art glass 'wearables.' These displays are useful to showcase your work in your home, at a craft exhibit or in a retail store showroom. As a bonus each of these displays is a unique work of art on its own and you may find people as interested in buying your display as they are in your jewelry.

Observations & Lessons

• A creative way to display glass jewelry
• Using glass rods

Additional Items

• Glass rods - COE 90, these rods are 3/16" (5 mm) in diameter x 15" (38 cm) long. (Note: Not all glass rods are COE 90, some are COE 33 made from borosilicate glass so be sure to get the correct ones)
• Plate stands, 2 per display rack - we used acrylic stands with a 3/16" (5 mm) slot

How It's Done

The overall size of the stands we made, as shown in the two photographs at left are approximately 11" (28 cm) wide x 14" (37 cm) tall. However, there is no need to make your stand the same size or even the same layout as the ones shown. My suggestion is to examine the finished stands in the photos to get a feel for how we did ours, then come up with a variation of your own.

1. The jewelry display stands shown in these two photos are very similar. The bottom clear piece of glass on the second display stand is a 4" x 11" (10 x 28 cm) rectangle with a concave curve in the top edge (we used a flexible-edge to draw the gentle curve, see photo 2 next page).

2. Assemble the display on a prepared kiln shelf. For this project I fired the clear glass and rod assembly directly on the KL board with a light dusting of kiln wash on it for the release. Use a nylon sock filled with kiln wash to sift a layer of dry kiln wash onto the board surface before starting the pre-fire assembly.

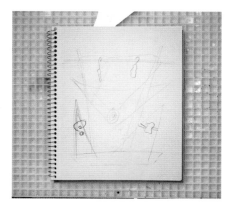

Pre-assemble The Displays

3. We are pre-assembling 2 different displays on one large KL board shelf that we can fit into our kiln and fire both at the same time. Place the bottom base glass on the KL board shelf, then lay 2 upright rods. Leave them as long as possible, but cut them to fit on the kiln shelf. Then cut and place 3 horizontal rods, leaving these rods long enough to extend on both sides.

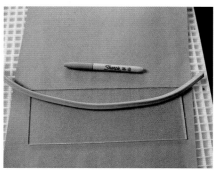

4. Because the rods are cylindrical, they roll and move around very easily. Place pieces of KL board or fiber blanket to create a stop, then place a drop of assembly glue at each intersection to hold the entire structure together.

5. Place the shelf with your stand in the kiln, then move the stops about 1/4" (6 mm) away from the rods. You could remove the stops altogether but I like to leave them, just in case the rods move after the glue fires off. If you leave them touching to the rod, they could create a dent or rough spots in the rod.

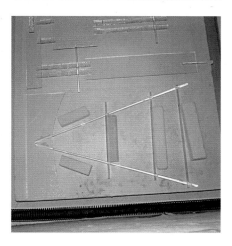

6. That's It! Close your kiln and fire the stand (or stands) using firing: **Schedule B - Medium - 1st Full Fuse**, on page 23.

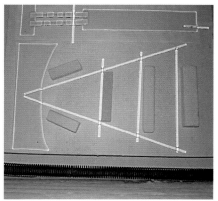

 Bonus

The stand shown in this photo was created to hang longer necklaces in addition to earrings. As you can see the design is radically different from the other 2 stands we created. This one uses rectangles and squares in addition to the glass rods. These glass rods are thin and are particularly well suited for hanging earrings and finger rings. However you certainly could create these stands without the rods and you could make them colored glass, although the idea is to keep the stand clear and let the jewelry have the 'star billing'. Another concept would be to design a stand that is custom made for a particular jewelry set (earrings, necklace, bracelet, rings, etc). Shape and position the various holders to custom fit the jewelry pieces and sell the whole unit (jewelry pieces and the stand) as a matched set.

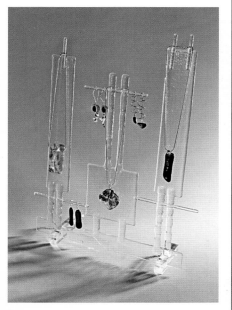

Wall Mirror Frame

Acontemporary furniture store in our town asked me to make a fused glass frame in a contemporary design then put a mirror in the frame to hang on a wall. I had never made a frame for a mirror before but it sounded like an interesting project and I was sure we could figure out how to do it. Let me say right now it is not possible to fuse mirror glass. Even if mirror had a compatible COE (which it doesn't) fusing temperatures would distort the glass and ruin the silver backing rendering the mirror useless. So the method we use is to create a fused frame and then glue the mirror to the frame from the back.

Our biggest challenge was to devise a clean and simple way to enable the mirror to hang. We either had to attach the hanging hardware to the frame or to the mirrored glass itself. For weeks we looked at the back of at least 100 mirrors in every kind of store imaginable and uncovered several possible solutions. Some were quite intricate and would have been costly to do while many others were either unattractive or unprofessional. So after some trials and tests we finally settled on a solution that makes use of a special mirror adhesive and readily available hanging hardware.

Observations & Lessons

- Designing with scissors
- Working with mirror glass
- A hanging system for a mirror
- Using glass shrinkage as a design element

Additional Items

- Adhesive: E-6000™, Mirror mastic, mirror edge sealant
- Picture hanger loops (2) and 18" (46 cm) of picture wire

How It's Done

1. As I mentioned previously, this mirror was intended for a contemporary furniture store so I wanted it to have an interesting shape, something more than just a rectangle. I started with a square piece of mirror glass and decided to cut an angled piece off the top, bottom and one side to eliminate all square (90°) corners.

2. Then I sat down with a paper and pencil and tried to conceive my frame design. I was not thrilled with any of the ideas I came up with until I remembered the knack to 'design with scissors'. I used some colored construction paper and cut out a few strips of various widths; 1/4" (6 mm), 1 1/2" (4 cm) and 2 1/2" (6 cm) wide. Then I trimmed, shaped, overlapped and arranged the strips until I came up with a design that I was happy with. I glued the pattern pieces together to make sure my design stayed put and also to give me a chance to step back to decide if I really liked it. The photo at the far right is my paper mock-up is sitting on top of the mirror glass.

3. OK so we're ready to start the cutting and glass assembly. Select the KL board shelf (or clay shelf) that will be the right size for your frame and cover it with a piece of thin release paper.

ProTip

Working With Mirror.
Always score mirror glass on the glass side, (this is the side you look into) not the coated side. Mirror is a very soft glass as compared to most stained glass and you'll need to be careful not to apply too much pressure when scoring (if you see chips popping off the glass surface after your score, you have pressed too much). Try to cut your mirror accurately by scoring and breaking. You want to avoid grinding the edge because it can chip the silver coating on the mirror back. A chipped edge is unsightly but more importantly it can speed up the corrosion that causes 'black edge'. You have probably seen mirrors with black spots along the edge. This happens when moisture and other corrosive substances damage the silver coating. The best way to prevent, or at least minimize this problem, is to protect the edge and the backside of the mirror with a spray sealant. Be sure to read the instructions on the sealant you choose and allow enough time for it to dry. Mirror scratches easily, especially the coated side and worse yet 'minor' scratches show up in a 'major' way on mirror. Be sure your work surface is clean before laying the mirror down to score it to avoid scratches on either side.

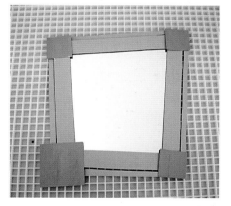

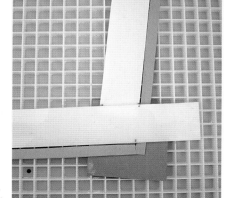

Choose & Cut The Glass

4. First cut four strips of white glass 1 1/2" x 12" (4 cm x 30 cm). Then cut four black squares, 3 are 2 1/2" (6 cm) and 1 is 3" (8 cm). Next cut four strips of red glass 1/4" x 12" (6 mm x 30 cm). Finally cut 4 strips of dichroic on black glass 1/4" x 6" (6 mm x 15 cm). Note: These sizes and colors reflect the choices that I made. Your frame could be any size or color that fits your artistic vision.

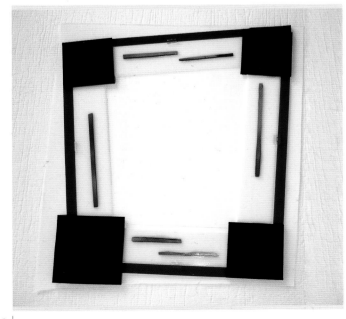

5. Start the assembly by placing one of the white strips on your paper pattern to mark and cut it to length. Do the same for the other 3 white pieces (Note: you can't see under the black iridized corner pieces in the photo but the white pieces do not overlap). Arrange the four white frame pieces on your kiln shelf then glue them to the release paper. Next trim and place the 1/4" (6 cm) red strips alongside the white strips, they should extend all the way to the corners and glue them to the thin release paper as well. Place and glue the black squares in each of the corners. Then add the dichroic glass but make sure not to place it too near the edges.

6. Now add a small piece of clear under the inside corner of the black squares and wherever you don't have two layers of glass. If you omit this step, your squares will shrink where there is no second layer and these edges will lose their even shape. By placing the white and the red strips side by side we are using the shrinkage of the single layer of glass as an interesting design element (see 3rd photo down on the next page). The tiny pieces of clear glass strategically placed are interrupting the open spaces.

7. Place the kiln shelf and assembly into your kiln and fire according to firing: **Schedule B - Medium - 1st Full Fuse**, on page 23.

8. Remove your frame from the kiln and clean off the release paper in the dunk-bucket.

Attach The Mirror To The Frame

9. For the final assembly attach the mirror to the frame using E-6000™ adhesive, clean the mirror and the frame with isopropyl alcohol first. Turn the frame face down, place some drops of adhesive at 16 or 20 spots around the inside edge (not too close that it will ooze out), carefully place the mirror (face down as well) onto the frame. Then let the E-6000™ set for 24 hours.

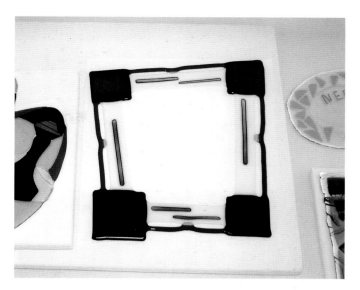

10. Our mirror has an uneven shape making it difficult to find the balanced center, so we decided to use two hangers versus one. But how to decide the location for two hangers when the top and bottom are uneven as well? Here is another handy use for the Morton System 'grid' surface. Place the mirror face down on the board. Position the mirror at the angle you would like it to hang (we chose a vertical alignment but a horizontal or a diamond configuration would work). Using the grid as your guide, place a long straight edge across the mirror back in the upper third of the mirror. Line it up with one of the grid lines and mark the two locations for the frame hangers. Attach the hangers using mirror mastic. This adhesive was specially formulated for use directly on mirror back coatings. It is important to use only mirror mastic as most other adhesives will cause the backing to corrode within a very short period of time. I also like to cut and attach a piece of cardboard to cover the back of the mirror, to more thoroughly protect the coating. Finally tie the picture-hanging wire between the two hooks for easy installation.

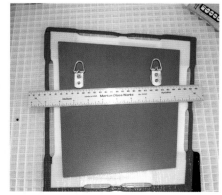

Wall Clock

The primary design element on this clock is pink and white 'Gestural Stringers' that we made using our flow system kiln, see Project 14 on page 94 for more information.

Screw-it pretty much describes how I got the idea for the assembly technique described in this chapter. We have not been very successful finding the appropriate local artisan to fabricate our wood or metal holders, mounting devices, frames, tables, stands and so on. The really skilled craftsmen are so busy that they are not accepting any new projects and the others just don't seem to be able to recreate our designs the way we envision them. We had tried so many things but were not happy with the results so we thought, "Screw It!" and went to the hardware store. Glass is quite sturdy and if it is designed and assembled in a particular way, it is not always necessary to have an accessory stand to hold it. For example if you drill holes and bolt (screw) two pieces together leaving a space between them, they can stand by themselves. This method opens a full range of possibilities to add dimension and depth to your glasswork without having to work with thick glass. (See Sculpture Gallery on page 67) 'Time is relative' and the timing couldn't be better to introduce this technique to you.

At first glance this project appears to be relatively simple. But this project is far from easy. Aside from the drilling and assembly to construct the 3-D clock the real lesson here is the technique to achieve an even and composed geometrical form using strips of glass versus the more common techniques of surface decorating a single layer base glass.

Observations & Lessons

- Constructing a geometrical shape from strips
- Screwing glass together to construct a 3D shape

Additional Items

- Clock Movement with threaded shaft at least 3/8" (9 mm) long, battery operated
- Hardware: Stainless steel - 2 round-head bolts 1/4" x 1 1/2" (6 mm x 4 cm), plus 4 standard hex nuts, 2 acorn nuts and two flat washers

How It's Done

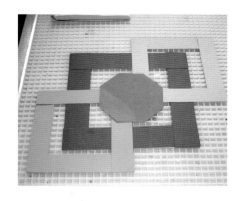

1. I like to create a full-size construction pattern mock-up for many of my projects to give me a chance to see if I like the shape and size. In addition to being the full-size pattern it will be used several times during the fabrication. Use the dimensions and fabrication instructions as listed in steps 3, 4, 8 & 9 to create your full-size mock-up or adapt the size of your clock to fit your kiln. When you are satisfied with your design, glue the pattern layout together and check to make sure it will fit completely within the boundaries of your kiln shelf.

2. I will admit that it is much easier for me to visualize a new design shape than it is to make new color choices. As you can probably tell from the projects in this book (and in my first book 'Introduction To Glass Fusing') I'm quite fond of a red, orange, yellow and green color palette. Or more accurately, red and any other color combination but I found out the hard way that some people *don't like red* (can you believe that?). So just to be different (for me anyway) I chose a new color palette for this project with light amber, dark amber and dark purple for the square frames and opalescent white for the center to hide the clock works. I liked this color combination so much that I used it again for Project 5 'Lazy Vase' (see page 46).

Creating The First Square

3. Begin by creating the bigger square that will be mounted at the back of the clock. Cut 4 strips in dark purple 2 1/4" x 12" (6 x 30 cm). Next cut 8 strips 3/4" x 9 1/2" (2 x 24 cm). If you have a Morton Portable Glass Shop this is a great opportunity to use it to score these strips with precision.

4. Clean each glass piece and place them on a prepared kiln shelf. We use shelf release paper which gives us the opportunity to glue the glass pieces directly to the paper. Position 2 strips parallel to one another and approximately 10" (25 cm) apart. Place the remaining 2 strips across the ends of the first strips so the ends are overlapping completely. Carefully straighten the edges and square the assembly. Use your full-size pattern mock-up as a guide to check your shape.

Preventing The Shrinkage Irregularity

5. We now have 2 layers of glass in the corners while the 'in between' areas are only a single layer. We know that full fusing will cause any single layer section to shrink, while two layers expand. To prevent this irregularity we will place 8 narrower strips along the edges in the single layer areas to make sure we have 2 layers of glass on all edges the entire way around. Note: Since this square is going to be taken to full fuse it is OK to put these narrower framing strips on top, even on the 2 sides that are placed on top of the other strips.

6. Clean all pieces, glue them together. Then place the shelf in the kiln and fire it according to: **Schedule B - Medium - 1st Full Fuse**, on page 23.

We placed 8 strips along the edges to make sure we had 2 layers of glass on all edges all the way around.

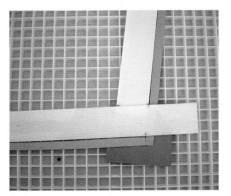

7. The upper section of the clock is a bit more complicated. Again we will need to have 2 layers of glass all the way around. This will ensure the edges will stay even and geometrically shaped.

8. We put a 6" (15 cm) diameter octagon in the center. (Here is another great opportunity to use your Morton Portable Glass Shop, great for cutting octagons). You could also cut a 6" (15 cm) square of white glass and cut off the corners to create an octagon.

9. Now cut 4 strips 1 1/2" x 9" x (4 x 23 cm) and 8 strips 1/2" x 5 1/2" (1.5 x 14 cm). Do this for each color (4 wide plus 8 narrow strips) of the light amber and the same for the dark amber. Clean each piece and set them aside for a moment.

Prepare The Central Clock Face

10. Prepare the center 'clock face' piece by placing clear support pieces under the white opal glass to create an even two layer piece. Place the glass as shown on the photo to the left on the back of the white glass. Now place a clear glass on top of that and draw one of the shapes with your glass marker (see photo left), score and break it out. Do this for each of the 4 support pieces. Clean the white face and the clear support glass, being careful to remove all the marker lines.

11. Next create some small glass pieces for the hour markers. We cut 4 bigger triangles in dark purple, 4 smaller triangles in light amber, another 4 small triangles in dark amber and glued them in place (see ProTip below for placement).

ProTip

If you think you are going to make more than this one clock in the future, we have this suggestion for a handy device you can make. It's a jig to help you locate the spots to glue the hour markers in the right place. We recycled a 4" (10 cm) metal jar lid and marked the 3, 6, 9, and 12 o'clock places with a long line and the other numbers with a dot. Now whenever we are making a clock we place this lid in the center of the glass and glue the number symbols around it.

Bonus

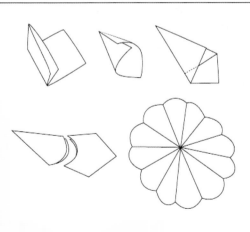

Another way to divide a circle into 12 equal pie shapes (at 30°) is to cut a piece of writing paper into a 6" (15 cm) square. Then fold it in half twice. Now for the tricky part, you have to fold both sides at the same time to make a 'one-third-pie' shape (see drawing). The last step is to round off the top of the pie and then open it to reveal 12 equally spaced creases for your marker spots. Flatten this 12-petal 'flower' and mark your clock face hours at each of the petal indents.

Pre-fuse Assembly

12. Now that all glass components are cut and cleaned we are ready to start the pre-fire assembly. This is a fairly large piece and we are using a single large piece of release paper on our KL board shelf. First we placed the release paper to the KL board then we laid the paper pattern on the release paper and traced the outline with a pencil. This pencil line will be the guide to position the glass pieces at the correct locations and angles.

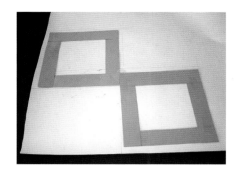

13. Start by placing the light and dark amber pieces for both of the square sections in the kiln. Use assembly glue to fasten them to the release paper. Place the clear supports in the center area then position the white octagon 'clock-face' with the hour markers already fastened in place and the clear glass on the back.

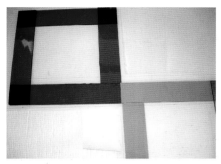

14. The final assembly step is to trim and place the narrower strips around the perimeter edges both inside and out. This will build up the single layer areas into 2 layers of glass on all edges, all the way around as we did for the 'bigger square' in steps 3 to 5.

15. Check your assembly to make sure everything is in the correct location and squared up the way you want it. Place the shelf in your kiln and fire it using: **Schedule B - Medium - 1st Full Fuse**, on page 23.

ProTip

      The task of moving the shelf board in and out of the kiln will be a lot easier if you place a few scrap pieces of KL board on the kiln floor before putting the shelf with glass assembly into the kiln.

16. The name of this project is 'Screw-It' and that is what we'll need to do to finish our clock. Start by washing the thin release paper off both glass sections. Mark the dead center of the clock face and place that entire section into your drilling tray. You'll need a shallow tray that is large enough to accommodate the largest fused glass section to about 1/4" (6 mm) underwater. Use your high-speed hand drill with a 5/16" (8 mm) hollow core drill bit to create the hole for the clock works. Note: Be sure to check the diameter of the shaft in your clock works - some require a 3/8" (9 mm) hole.

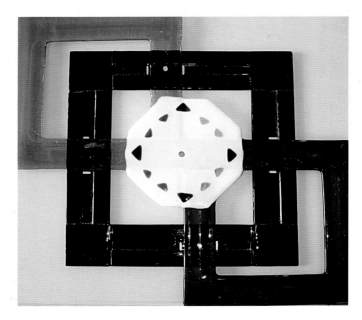

17. Drill 2 holes using a 1/4" (6 mm) hollow core drill bit. Place the larger dark purple square on top of the clock face section and carefully center it. Mark the location for the holes at the intersections on both the left and right side (see photo at left). Place this purple square in the drilling tray and drill both holes.

18. Place the purple square back on the clock face section and transfer the location for the holes by marking through both holes with your glass marker. Place the clock face section in the drilling tray and drill both remaining holes.

Screw-It All Together

19. The final assembly step is to 'screw-it' all together. We started to assemble the clock with the purple square at the back as in photo one liked the layout of the purple glass one top

20. Push the 1 1/2" (4 cm) long, round-head bolts up through the holes from the bottom of the purple square section. Screw one of the hex nuts onto each bolt but do not tighten them, allowing the bolts to move around slightly. Screw the other hex nut onto each bolt until you have about 1/2" (1.5 cm) of the treads showing. Now pick up the clock face section and carefully position it onto the bolts. If necessary you can move the bolts slightly to line them up with the holes (that's why you didn't tighten them fully). Screw the acorn nuts onto each bolt and tighten those down. Finally use a pair of pliers to snug all four hex nuts down onto the glass. But be careful! The nuts only need to be 'snug,' do not heavily tighten them or you will risk cracking the glass. Place a washer between the hex nut and the glass.

21. Install the clock works by pushing the shaft through the hole in the face section and screw on the hex nut (provided in the clock works kit). Install the clock hands onto the clock shaft and insert a battery. Set the correct time of day and enjoy your new clock!

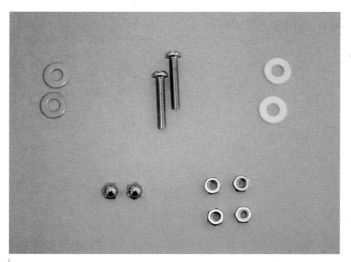

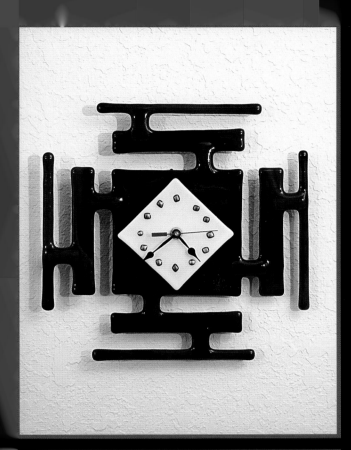

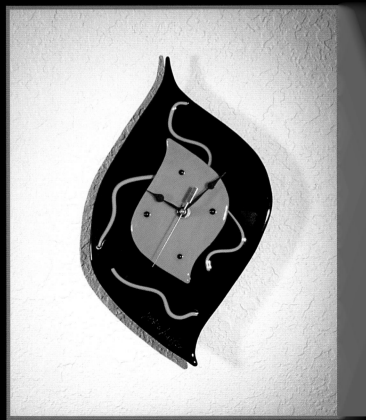

Lazy Vase

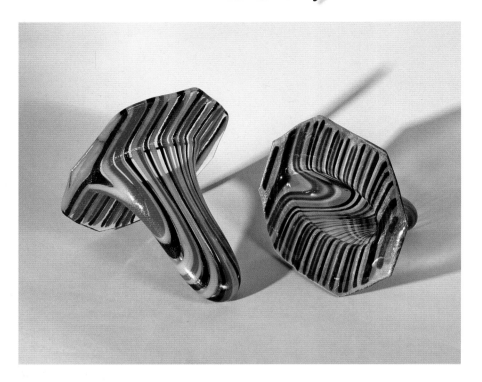

Wait - not on the floor! By 'Drop It' we mean to heat the glass up until it drops through the opening of a 'drop out mold.' In the drop out process the glass is heated just to the point where it begins to drop or more specifically be 'drawn down' by gravity under its own weight. Several years ago I attended a gallery exhibit with many stunning vases created using this technique. The artist obviously had mastered the technique of 'dropping' the glass, confirmed by the consistent thickness of the walls in each of the vases. To get really first-rate results you must be very patient with your glass, keep a watchful eye and carefully control the firing schedule.

In order to keep the sides from getting too thin during the drop, we will need a relatively thick pre-fired glass blank for this project. We can create a thick blank that also has an interesting pattern by cutting 1/4" (6 mm) wide strips of glass from several different colors, Then stand the strips together on edge on a clear glass base. The center area of the blank will fire down to the equivalent thickness of 3 glass layers approximately 3/8" (9 mm). Then we will fire the prefused blank on the dropout mold to create the vase and 'stop the drop' (by flashing the kiln) just before the glass bottom hits the kiln shelf. You can tell by looking at this vase that it is not designed to stand up on its bottom. Instead it is to be displayed in a 'laying down' position - hence the name 'Lazy Vase.'

Observations & Lessons

- Dropout (or drop through) firing process
- Multi-color 'strip' design technique
- An out-of-the-ordinary method for making ultra-thin glass shards

Additional Items

- Old kitchen butter knife or a small saw to create the mold cutout

How It's Done

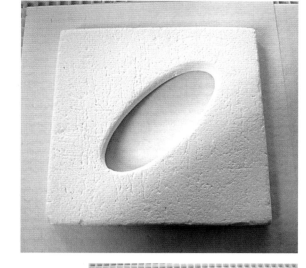

1. Dropout 'ring-molds' are available in clay and stainless steel in a variety of sizes. However we prefer to make our own size and shape using Kaiser Lee Board. Our favorite dropout mold is an oval cut into an 8" x 9" x 1" thick (20 x 23 x 2.5 cm) piece of KL board. Create a cardboard pattern for the oval shape using the oval that is under-printed in the background on this page. Place the oval diagonally on the KL board, being careful to center it and then trace the outline with a pencil.

2. Use a small saw (or kitchen knife) to cut and remove the oval from the center. Be very gentle when cutting KL board, the knife will slice through easily. It is essential to cut straight down perpendicular to avoid any undercuts angles that could hinder the release of the glass when forming.

Choose & Cut The Glass

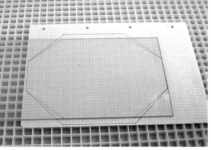

3. If you are using clear iridescent glass for the base of your blank as we are be sure to place it iridescent side down on your KL board kiln shelf. Using iridescent glass there is no need to kiln wash or use release paper. However, if your base glass is non-iridized or if you are using a clay drop out mold you will need to apply a mold release.

4. Cut and shape the (clear iridescent) glass you selected for the base. To fit on the mold, you'll need a base glass that is 2" (5 mm) larger than the oval mold opening.

5. Next cut a variety of 1/4" (6 mm) wide strips using your selections of colored glass. You could use a ruler, mark off the strips then score and break them. But it's so much more fun, not to mention easier and faster, to use a tool that is specially made for this task. There are several strip-cutting devices available (the Morton Portable Glass Shop is shown in the photos), be sure to ask your friendly glass retailer to make a recommendation. The strips are going to be positioned side-by-side and standing on edge. When you think you have enough strips cut, lay a kiln post down on your bench, lean the first strip against it, then continue to stack the strips in a pleasing pattern (try putting several pieces of the same color together to create a wider color bar). When your stack is approximately 2" (5 mm) shorter than the length of the base glass, anchor the other end with a 2nd kiln post (the kiln posts are only temporary).

> **ProTip**
> When the glass drops through the form it is actually stretching the glass. The deeper the drop, the thinner the glass will become. If the glass is too thin it cannot be used and that's why it's important to work with a thicker glass blank and be very patient with your firing schedule. A good rule of thumb is to use 1 layer of standard thick glass 1/8" (3 mm) per 2" (5 cm) of drop depth. We plan to set this mold up on 7" (18 cm) kiln posts and drop the vase in this project down 6" (15 cm). That means we would need to use 3 layers of glass for a 3/8" (10 mm) blank or the equivalent thickness using the strip technique.

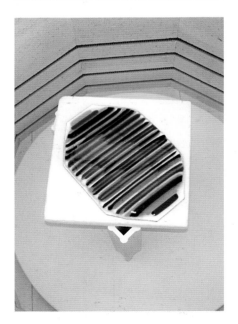

6. Now cut the strips to length, leaving a 3/4" (2 cm) border rim around the perimeter of the base glass. Begin by cleaning the base glass and laying it iridescent side down on the KL board kiln shelf (or a prepared standard shelf). Make a glass 'start point anchor' using two glass strips. Cut each piece leaving the 3/4" (2 cm) wide border rim in from the base glass edge (that means you need to cut them 1 1/2" (4 cm) shorter). Secure the two anchor pieces flat side down using a few drops of assembly glue. This anchor will support your strip stack as you build it in place. Now one by one pull a strip in order from your pre-build stack, mark and cut it to length, clean it and add it to the new stack. Finish the other end with another 'end point anchor.'

Fire The Vase Blank

7. Carefully place the shelf in your kiln and fire according to: **Schedule C - Large - 1st Full Fuse**, on page 23.

8. When the blank is cooled down, remove it from the kiln and clean it in the dunk bucket. Grind off any spikes or rough edges with an abrasive stone and make sure the glass blank still fits on your mold.

9. The final step is the dropout firing. Prepare the kiln by placing a shelf in the kiln. If the dropout gets a little out of hand and the glass reaches the floor, the shelf with release paper, or fiber paper will save the vase (and your kiln floor). Place three 7" (18 cm) kiln posts in the kiln and balance the dropout mold on top of them. Carefully adjust the posts to eliminate any interference with the glass when it drops through the opening. Position your prefused blank on top of the mold, being sure to center it over the opening. Program and fire your kiln according to: **Schedule G - Medium Large - Deep Drop**, on page 23.

Start The Dropout Firing

10. A dropout firing is a little bit more complicated than a standard slump or drape firing. The glass blank is fairly thick plus it is suspended in the center of the kiln and that means you need to be extra careful during the ramp-up phase. I have had consistently good results using a ramp-up speed of 5°F (3°C) per minute.

11. The other problem in a dropout firing is the operator's own patience during the drop phase. The ramp up is slow and when the drop finally begins it also goes verrrrry slooooowly. In the same length of time it takes to go from 'lovely brown toast to nasty burnt toast' the glass will begin to drop quite rapidly and if you are not on top of the firing, the piece can easily drop too fast - stretching and thinning the sidewalls. When the kiln has reached 1000°F (538°C) the first ramp-up phase is complete and the temperature will steadily increase.

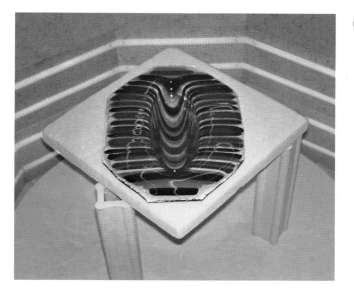

ProTip

Glass artists with a good deal more patience than me, say they program their kilns to hold for several hours at a slow dropping temperature in the range of 1250°F (677°C), anywhere from 4 to 8 hours (the optimum temperature for this will vary from kiln to kiln so do some experiments to find the correct temperature for your kiln). They claim this extended hold-drop method promotes a thicker wall and lessens the possibility of a molten disaster on the kiln floor, it's worth a try!

12. When the kiln reaches 1280°F (693°C) begin to keep a very close watch. This is the time to diligently observe your piece (See Bonus tip below) when it has dropped about 2" (5 cm). Slow down the stretch a bit by opening and closing the lid (3 to 5 seconds only) to lower the temperature, no more than 20°F (7°C) as you don't want to stop the drop completely. Continue to closely observe the drop, allowing it to flow freely but not too rapidly. Remember, you can stop the drop at any time by flashing the kiln down to 1200°F (649°C). I like to stop my Lazy Vase just before it hits the bottom shelf. But this is your piece, you're the artist so make your own creative decision.

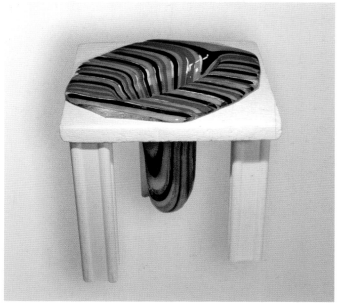

Bonus

Paper Thin Glass Shards
Set up your drop out mold but this time use a single sheet of glass only (not a thick blank). Fire it to ramp up at 15°F (9°C) per minute to 1300°F (700°C) and hold. Let it drop deep but be sure to stop it before it hits the kiln floor. The drop through glass will get very, very thin. When it has cooled, carefully remove it from the mold as it can break easily. Place it between several layers of newspaper and hit

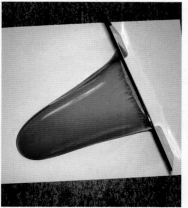

the lower thin part lightly with a block of wood to break it up. The resulting 'thin shards' can be used to enhance and decorate many fused projects. Think of it as custom 'fractured' glass. Create a selection of fracture colors and store them in a multi compartment case for easy retrieval. Be sure to make the COE number on the case.

Bonus! Bonus Tip: Pre-fuse a glass blank using multiple colors or dichroic glass with the full fused to a single layer schedule and deep drop that blank to get multicolored glass shards.

Indoor Fountain

Knowing Fish (A Zen Narrative - author unknown) One day Chuang Tzu and a friend were walking by a river. "Look at the fish swimming about," said Chuang Tzu, "They are really enjoying themselves." "You are not a fish," replied the friend, "So you can't truly know that they are enjoying themselves." "You are not me," said Chuang Tzu. "So how do you know that I do not know that the fish are enjoying themselves?"

Watch the water bubble up through the layers of fused glass and hear it cascading down into the pool of water. These soothing water sounds, combined with the mesmerizing look of the cascading water, makes for a calm, relaxing 'Zen-like' experience.

Observations & Lessons

- Create a tabletop fountain
- Achieve a 'wet look' effect on glass
- Produce a 2" (5 cm) deep-drop bowl
- Kiln carve glass using fiber paper

Additional Items

- Fountain pump; not higher than 2" (5 cm) with adjustable water flow control, plus a 2" (5 cm) length of clear vinyl tube that fits on the pump discharge tab

How It's Done

While working on this fountain design I considered a variety of complex shapes and contraptions trying to design something clever and dramatic for this book. For some reason I kept coming back to this design. Once you understand the basic fountain building process you can let your imagination soar to take your fountain design to the next level.

Fountain Basin Bowl – First Things First

It's a good idea to create the basin bowl portion of the fountain first. This will give us a chance to measure and confirm the exact sizes for the other components in the fountain including the cascading tiles. We'll create the basin as you would any other bowl. Flat-fused a blank with a minimum of 2 layers of glass then slump the blank into a 2" deep drop out mold to shape the fountain pool.

1. The drop out mold was made from a 14" (36 cm) square piece of KL board - using the 1" (2.5 cm) thick material. Measure and mark a 9" (23 cm) square in the center and cut that section out using a stainless steel putty knife (or a kitchen knife) to create a mold with a 2 1/2" (6 cm) wide border frame (see photo top right on page 19).

2. Next make the flat fused blank. Cut a 13" (33 cm) square of plum iridescent glass and a 13" (33 cm) square of clear glass. Clean both pieces and place the plum glass iridescent side down on a KL board kiln shelf. Iridescent glass will not stick to a KL board shelf so you don't need kiln wash or any other separator. If your not using iridescent glass (or a KL board kiln shelf) or if you want the bottom surface of the bowl to be a little smoother, you should cover the shelf with a layer of thin release paper. Then place the plum glass down first with the clear glass on top.

3. Use mosaic cutters to break some clear glass (use scrap pieces) into small irregularly shaped chunks approximately 3/8" (1 cm). Place these pieces randomly on the top layer of your unfired glass blank (leave an area in the center open). This simple technique will produce an interesting texture that is reminiscent of a wet or icy surface.

4. Place the whole assembly into your kiln and fire it following: **Schedule C - Large - 1st Full Fuse**, on page 23. Note: Since the top layer of glass is a single large piece of glass you may want to perform a 'bubble squeeze' soak during the target up phase of the firing, see page 24 for more information on this process.

Fountain Basin - Dropout Slump

5. Place the drop out mold (that you created in step 1) on a fiberboard shelf in your kiln. Then lift the mold off the shelf by placing 1" (2.5 cm) kiln post risers under it on all 4 sides (be sure the risers will not interfere with the glass as it drops through the mold). The glass will slump through the opening to create a 2" (5 cm) total drop, 1" (2.5 cm) for the mold thickness and 1" (2.5 cm) for the riser. Now position and center your flat fused blank on top of the mold (iridescent side down of course). If you're not using iridescent glass you should cover the mold with a sheet of thin release paper before placing down the glass blank.

6. Slump fire your fountain basin according to: **Schedule F - Medium/Large - Slump**, on page 23.

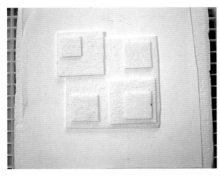

Fountain Cascading Tiles

7. We'll create two tiles that will produce a gentle cascade of water into the basin. For the first tile we'll need one piece of clear glass 8" (20 cm) square, one piece of mauve opalescent glass 7" (18 cm) square and 4 clear glass strips 1/2" x 7 1/2" (1.5 cm x 19 cm). Clean the glass and build your assembly on a kiln shelf in the following order; thin release paper, clear glass square, mauve opalescent glass square (centered on the clear) and finally place the clear strips around the outer edge of the mauve glass, Secure everything with a little assembly glue.

8. The second tile is created in the same way except it will be 1" (2.5 cm) smaller. Cut one piece of clear glass 7" (18 cm) square, one piece of iridescent purple cathedral (transparent) glass 6" (15 cm) square and 4 clear glass strips 1/2" x 6 1/2" (1.5 cm x 16 mm). Assemble these pieces as described in step 7 and be sure to secure everything with glue.

9. Next we'll create 4 square nuggets that we'll use as spacers to separate the cascade tiles during final fountain assembly. Cut 8 pieces of clear and 4 pieces of opalescent purple glass all 1" (2.5 cm) square. Stack them on the same shelf as the tile (if you have room) in the following order; thin release paper, 1 clear square, 1 purple square and another clear square. Create these stacks for all 4 nuggets.

10. If your kiln shelf is large enough to hold all these components you will place and fire them all in one firing. Fire the kiln according to: **Schedule B - Medium - 1st Full Fuse**, on page 23.

Kiln Carving Glass Using Fiber Paper

11. We'll 'kiln carve' 4 square compartments into the surface of the uppermost cascade tile (the smaller of the two tiles). These indents will be used to confine 4 glass marbles, allowing the marbles to move about as the water flows around them. You will need a 4" (10 cm) square piece of 1/16" (1.5 mm) thick fiber paper and several smaller squares (we used 6) in assorted sizes (see photo). Place an 8" (20 cm) square of thin release paper on your kiln shelf and glue the 4" (10 cm) square fiber paper in the center. Now arrange and glue the 6 smaller fiber paper pieces to the 4" (10 cm) square fiber paper in a similar pattern to what you see in the photo.

HotTip

In the 'Observations & Lessons' section at the opening of this project we mentioned 'Kiln carve glass using fiber paper'. Kiln carving simply involves placing a cutout shape of fiber paper between the kiln shelf and a glass blank. Then fire the glass until it forms around this piece of fiber paper creating an indent that will be the same shape as the fiber paper cutout. This indent is essentially a 'carved out' space in the surface of the glass - hence the name 'Kiln Carving'. You can use other media for kiln carving, such as chunks of fiberboard or draw a pattern using thick kiln wash powder. Or create a shape using copper wire, make a tracery of sand or arrange some stones, remember to cover these items with a sheet of thin release paper.

12. Place the smaller tile on top of the fiber paper mold iridescent side down. Place everything in your kiln and fire according to: **Schedule B - Medium - 1st Full Fuse**, on page 23. **Note: the ramp up speed must be slowed down to 5°F (3°C) per minute**, since this tile has already been flat fuse fired. When the kiln has cooled, remove the carved tile and pick the fiber paper pieces out of the indents.

Assemble The Fountain

13. Drill a hole in the center of both cascade tiles large enough to accommodate the pump tube. Use your high-speed hand drill with a 1/2" (1.3 cm) hollow core drill bit (or whatever diameter you need to match your pump tube). Mark the center of the tiles and place them one at a time into your drilling tray, make sure the tile is about 1/8" (3 mm) underwater.

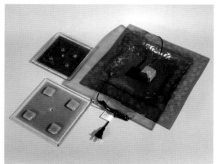

14. Finally assemble the fountain. First mount a short length of the clear vinyl tube, about 3" (8 cm) on the pump's discharge tab then place the pump in the bottom of the basin bowl. Thread the pump tube through the hole in the bigger tile and seat it on top of the pump. Then arrange the 4 nuggets on it and place the smaller 'carved' tile over the tube to rest on the nuggets. Mark and cut the excess length of the vinyl tube to make it flush with the top of the upper tile. Fill the bowl with clean water and turn on the pump. Adjust the water flow (an adjustment dial is on the pump) so it bubbles up about 1" (2.5 cm) and cascades gracefully over the tiles.

15. The final flourish is to place the marbles (or glass beads) into the carved indents in the upper most tile. These little compartments will hold the marbles while allowing them to add

ProTip

If you have ever owned an indoor fountain you have probably experienced how dirty it can become over a short time. We created our first fused glass fountain with the idea that glass would be easier to keep clean than stone or other more porous material. But after we left it in a gallery on consignment for 3 months we realized just how wrong we were. We have since learned how to take care of our fountain and it is not that difficult. Simply run it daily, make sure it has enough water and once a week add a few drops of chlorine bleach or algae controller. Then take it apart once a month or so to clean the components with dishwashing detergent. Otherwise, you could use commercially available indoor fountain water treatments to control algae growth and scale buildup.

Ambiance Light

When I dreamed up this project I thought it was a completely original idea. But a few months after I made my first one I noticed a similar lamp at the John C. Campbell Folk School gift shop in North Carolina. My Ambiance Light was not exactly the same and you could tell the designs were developed independently but it reinforces the theory that 'nothing is entirely new in this world.' We've given this lamp a permanent spot in our motor home to enjoy when we travel and it really enhanced the ambiance in the room - and that is why we named it 'Ambiance.'

A fascinating feature of this project is the use of non fusible glass for the entire project. How'd we do that? Well we found an interesting sheet of handrolled glass and used glass from *that sheet only* for the project.

Observations & Lessons

- Drape both a lamp base and a lampshade
- Lamp fixture fabrication and installation
- Create a kiln object with non tested compatible glass

Additional Items

- Lamp Parts (candelabra light kit) including: 1 Threaded nipple - 3/4" (2 cm), 2 Brass lock nuts, 1 Brass washer, 3 Rubber (or plastic) washers, 1 Mini-base bulb socket, 1 Power cord with inline switch

How It's Done

1. The base of this lamp is a single layer of glass draped over a simple mold. I picked through my collection of assorted KL board pieces left over from previous projects (I never throw away any pieces). The larger piece is about 4" (10 cm) square and the smaller piece is 2 1/2" (6 cm) square (it's a different color because it was previously coated with primer). I used a sanding block to round the upper edges and corners on both mold pieces. This will produce smooth corners on the draped glass base and will make extraction of the mold pieces easier.

2. Cut a piece of glass 7" (18 cm) square and cut a piece of thin release paper 8" (20 cm) square. Place a shelf in the kiln and stack the mold pieces on it as shown in the photo on page 55. Cover the mold with the sheet of thin release paper then balance the glass on the mold. I turned my glass slightly on the mold to offset the square and add a point of interest to the overall design.

This is what the bottom side of the base looked like after the drape firing.

Lamp Base Slump Firing

3. Fire the kiln following: **Schedule E - Medium/Large - Drape**, on page 23. Note: Increase the target hold time to 15 or 20 minutes to allow the glass to conform more closely to the mold shape and to fire polish the bottom edge at the same time.

4. After firing, carefully extract the mold pieces. Try to keep them intact in one piece for future use. Soak the glass in your dunk bucket to remove the thin release paper residue.

5. The lampshade section requires 2 separate kiln firings, one to full-fuse the flat blank and one to drape it over a mold. Cut the following glass pieces: 1 pc - 5" (13 cm) square, 4 pcs - 1" x 5" (2.5 x 13 cm), 4 pcs - 1" x 2" (2.5 x 5 cm), 4 pcs - 1" (2.5 cm) square. Clean and dry all the glass pieces in preparation for pre-fire assembly.

Pre-fuse Assembly

6. We'll assemble the glass for this full-fuse flat blank on a 12" (30 cm) square KL board shelf. Cover the KL board with thin release paper and use a little assembly glue to fasten the 5" (13 cm) square glass to the center of the paper. Next center the 1" (2.5 cm) squares along each side of the square glass and glue them to the paper as well. Then glue the 5" (13 cm) strips next to the squares, parallel to the main square piece of glass. The final and very important assembly step is to glue the 2" (5 cm) strips across the joints - from the outer glass strips to the center square piece. You should have 1/2" (1.5 cm) extending past the joint on either end of these joiner pieces. This is an important step as the little one-inch squares will give the construction stability and keep the width of the bridge constant otherwise this joiner glass would shrink if it was only one layer thick.

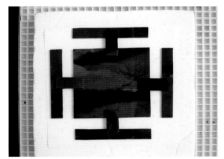

7. Set the kiln shelf on your kiln floor and fire using: **Schedule B - Medium - 1st Full Fuse**, on page 23. When the kiln has cooled, remove the blank and clean it by submerging it in your dunk bucket to remove the release paper, then dry it thoroughly.

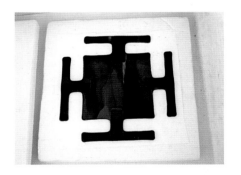

8. Now prepare the drape mold for the lampshade. We made our mold using 2" (5 cm) thick KL board. You could build a mold using the 1" (2.5 cm) thick material, by stacking several 2" (5 cm) square pieces on top of each other. Secure this stack using a 5 1/2" (14 cm) stainless steel spike pushed up from the bottom. Another alternative would be to use one of the 6" (16 cm) high 'Floral Vase' stainless steel slump molds (available from fusing suppliers). These molds are cylindrical and tapered from 2" (5 cm) at the top, to 3" (8 cm) at the bottom but would work out just fine for this project. See ProTip on page 61 for more information on this stainless steel Floral Vase draper mold.

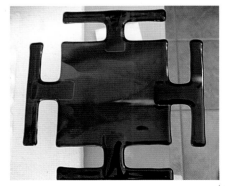

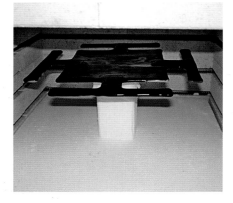

Drape Fire The Lampshade

9. Cover the top of the prepared drape mold with a piece of pre-fired fiber paper - this recycled material is soft and pliable. The fiber paper cap will allow the glass to release from the mold easier and the inside bottom of the lampshade will be smoother.

10. Place the mold in the kiln and make sure it doesn't rock or move. Then center and balance the flat-fired blank on the mold (we used a ruler to ensure we had it in the center). Fire your kiln using: **Schedule E - Medium/Large - Drape**, on page 23.

11. Using a 13/32" (1 cm) hollow core drill bit in a high speed rotary tool to drill a hole in the center of the lampbase and also in the center of lampshade. Remember to submerge your glass in water, with a second piece of flat glass under it before drilling. Finally use your grinder to create a little groove in the bottom edge of the lampbase to create a place for the electric cord to come out.

12. Assemble the components and the electrical fixture. Follow these steps in order.

- Screw one of the lock nuts about 1/4" (6 mm) down onto the nipple. Place the brass washer on the nipple (from the longer side), then one of the rubber washers, then push the nipple up from the bottom (inside) of the lampbase.

- Put the other rubber washer over the nipple then place the lampshade on it, another rubber washer and secure the whole thing with the another lock nut. This part is a bit tricky because the space inside the shade is small, try using flat nose pliers but be careful that you don't over tighten the nut.

- Thread the cord up from the bottom through the nipple and pull it through until it is about 6" (15 cm) above the lampshade.

- Install the wires into the socket (according to the instructions that came with your fixture kit). Gently pull down on the cord until the socket is seated against the nipple then screw the socket onto the nipple until it is tight.

13. That's it! Screw in a light bulb, plug it in and enjoy.

Showcase Gallery

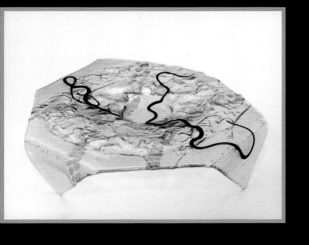

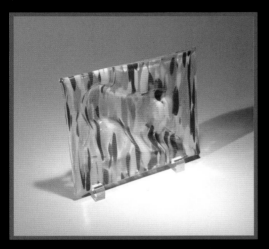

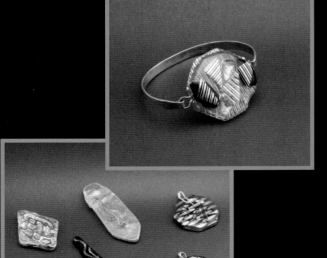

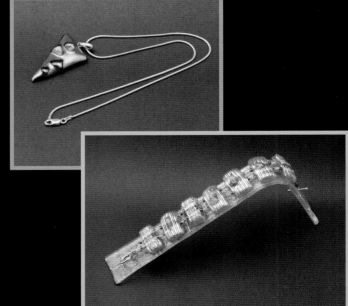

Lesson 8 - Drape It
Pendant Chandelier

It is not that I don't like blown glass, I do... really! Unfortunately kiln worked glass isn't always held with the same high esteem even though it can be just as interesting and challenging. I'll bet you have seen those beautiful light pendant chandeliers, they are turning up everywhere, even in the giant home centers. Most are made using imported blown glass shades, so I thought; "What if we made them out of fused and formed glass?"

I didn't anticipate just how challenging it would be to come up with a workable design. You have the advantage of seeing my final creation and you may wonder; what was so challenging about that? I will show you some of my experiments and dilemmas as you follow along this project. You will see how one thing leads to another and learn how an unexpected result can often guide your creativity in a new direction for future projects.

Observations & Lessons

- Test & correction designing
- Choose the right colors
- Kiln carving with fiber paper
- Making and using a drape mold

Additional Items

- Lamp Parts: Pendant light kits are available at most local hardware stores and are less expensive than purchasing individual parts. We purchased one of the triple pendant light chandeliers (from one of the giant home centers) and replaced the imported lampshade with our new glass pendant shade.

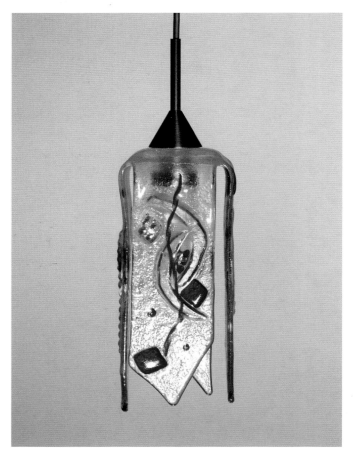

How It's Done

When I sat down to figure out what this pendant lampshade would consist of, I found I had a few decisions to make. Was I going to make these shades with the drape technique as we did in Project 7 "Ambiance Light", or would I use the deep-drop technique as we did in Project 5 "Lazy Vase". A shade made in the deep drop style would have a large flat rim that would actually be the bottom edge in this inverted hanging lamp. A deep-drop style could have worked but it wasn't really what I had envisioned for my light pendant.

I decided the drape technique would likely produce the best results. So, I conducted a couple of experiments using some non tested-compatible glass (only because this glass is less expensive). The photos here at right show the end results of the first two samples I created.

Test Drape #1

Test Drape #1.

This started out as a 10" (25 cm) square piece of glass that I draped over the same 2" x 2" x 8" (5 x 5 x 20 cm) KL board mold that we used for the Ambiance Light, in step 8 on page 55. I liked it but the shape was a bit too ordinary for what I wanted. However with some creative decoration this could become a very nice shade. I'm currently using it as a pencil holder on my desk.

Test Drape #2.

This started out as an 8" x 12" (20 x 30 cm) rectangle with slightly rounded off ends. I draped it over a 6" x 6" (15 x 15 cm) square, 1" (2.5 cm) thick KL board mold standing on edge. It certainly is an interesting shape but not one that is well suited for a pendant shade, however I discovered a great way to create a new bowl shape.

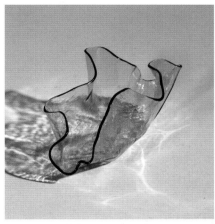

Test Drape #2

Now What?

The first two experiments were very useful because they forced me to rethink the idea of a one piece, flat blank shape. I decided to make a mock up using colored construction paper and I started by making a cross from 2" x 16" (5 x 40 cm) wide strips of paper. I tacked them at the center and bent them over my 2" x 2" x 8" (5 x 5 x 20 cm) KL board mold. Now we had something! I decided right there and then that this was the one, so I began to create a fully decorated version (no experimental version this time). You can see my first and final creation all wired up and mounted on the preceding page at bottom left.

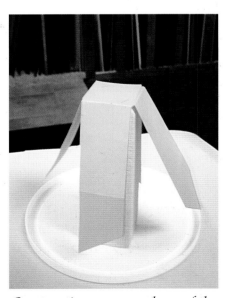

Construction paper mock-up of the final pendant shade shape

> ### ProTip
> Attempting to maintain precision control over the final shape and appearance of kiln formed glass can be challenging, especially if you're trying to make exact repeat copies of a particular design or shape. The best way to deal with this issue is to make some subtle differences on purpose, or expect subtle differences will happen, then accept them as a gift. I have always found these differences add interest and certainly uniqueness to my creations.

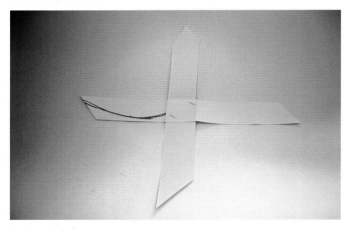

1. Choose or create the drape mold. We made our mold from a piece of 2" (5 cm) thick KL board. It is 2" x 2" x 8" (5 x 5 x 20 cm) and will be used standing on one end. We rounded off the side corners and the top rim using a sanding block then coated all sides with liquid mold release (1 part release with 6 parts water). See ProTip below for more information on mold release.

2. Once you have selected and prepared your mold you need to determine the exact size for the glass by creating a full-size paper pattern, ours is 16" x 16" (40 x 40 cm). Place the paper pattern over your mold and loosely fold it to simulate how the glass will fall during the drape. Check the length of each arm as well as the overall shape.

3. Take a look at the layout of our flat blanks and you will notice that we cut the end of each arm at an angle (third photo on the right). We did this for two reasons. Putting an angle on the ends adds some design interest to the finished shade and as a side benefit lessens the need for a precision slump. When you are satisfied with the shape and size of your paper shade, use it to cut your 2 component glass parts.

4. We chose clear iridescent glass for the base and some small pieces of red, amber and dichroic/clear for the design. Firing the glass iridescent side down will give an interesting effect to the surface and since we are using a KL board kiln shelf, the iridescent surface will not stick to it. We used two different surface decorating techniques that we will describe.

ProTip

Glass drapes around 1200°F to 1250°F (649°C to 677°C). At this temperature, mold release (kiln wash) will not stick to glass so we like to use regular kiln wash to give the board a nice smooth surface (rather than the hi-temp release that turns to dust during firing). Please be aware that the board will heavily soak up the liquid the first time you apply kiln wash and it will need a longer time to dry. We often do several molds at once and leave them to air dry for up to 1 week, however you can speed the drying by placing it in a warm kiln for a few hours until it has dried completely.

Kiln Carving With Fiber Paper

5. The first surface decorating technique is 'Kiln Carving with Fiber Paper.' This design technique is one of my favorites due to the subtle yet effective markings that it produces. Cut some fiber paper shapes and glue them to the iridescent (bottom) side of the glass with assembly glue. We created curves and crescent moon shapes for these lampshades. After firing, the paper is removed leaving a carved-like relief in the glass surface. Place your glass pieces iridescent side down on the kiln shelf. Center the cross pattern then glue it together to ensure it stays centered.

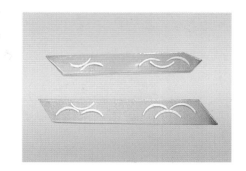

6. The second surface decorating technique I love to do is use our own 'homemade' dual colored glass stingers (see Project 14 'Gestural Strings Of Glass' on page 84). We've strategically placed stringers and some dichroic pieces on this shade to carefully add understated color, to enhance but not overpower the kiln carvings.

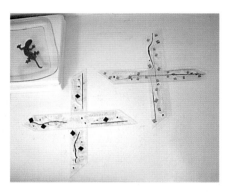

7. Place the shelf in your kiln and fire it using: **Schedule B - Medium - 1st Full Fuse**, on page 23.

The Drape Firing

8. Place the 2" x 2" x 8" (5 x 5 x 20 cm) mold in the center of your kiln then balance the flat-fused blank cross on top of it. Fire using: **Schedule E - Medium/Large - Drape**, on page 23.

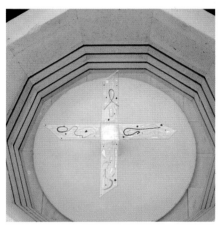

9. The final step is to drill a hole in the top of each lampshade to accommodate the electric light fixture, then wire each shade. Be sure to carefully consider the length of the cord with respect to the effect you want the final installation to have.

ProTip

Stainless Steel 'Floral Former' or 'Vase Draper'
This stainless steel drape mold is commonly referred to as a 'Floral Former'. The name is derived from the flower-like shapes that are created when the glass is draped over it. We used a floral former mold to create the simple lampshade shown at far right. We coated the outside of the stainless steel canister with boron nitride as our separator (a liquid release that is applied with a hake brush). Be sure to read 'Surface Preparation For Stainless Steel' on page 63 and 'Stainless Steel (formed sheet metal)' on page 16 for more information on stainless steel

surface preparation. After the mold was ready we simply cut a 12" (30 cm) circle from a white iridized opal glass, centered it on the mold and fired it using: **Schedule E - Medium/Large - Drape**, on page 23. Once the shade had cooled we drilled a hole using a 13/32" (1 cm) hollow core drill bit in the high speed rotary drill. Then used a swag lamp kit to wire it up for an accent shade.

The Wave

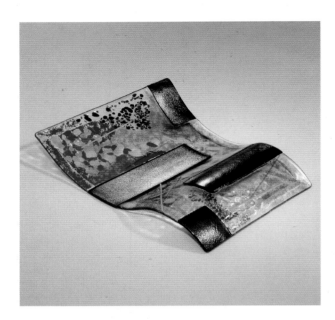

Airport Gridlock! - Here's The Back-story

I design most of my pieces without a background story but I wanted to create something a little more substantive for this sculpture so I looked for a theme. We were on our way home after attending the Las Vegas Glass Craft and Bead Expo. The cab dropped us at the airport, where we lined up at the curb to check our bags. We entered the airport terminal and made our way toward the security checkpoint only to find six huge lines of people moving slowly, endeavoring to wedge themselves into a single long line. The crowd began zig zagging their way around barriers and following along railings. We joined the throng of people and shuffled for nearly three hours until we passed through security. Anxiety, frustration, powerless, cynicism, all mixed with a curious feeling of understandable necessity, these were just some of the moods we were able to observe, both in ourselves and in the huge crowd around us. I tried to express this experience of the multitude of people (represented by the frit) merging around the barriers (the black blocks) to eventually be combined into one (the fuse).

Observations & Lessons

- Preparing a stainless steel mold for firing
- Methods for making glass frit
- Working with glass frit
- Create a distinctive line using reverse firing
- Intensify iridescent glass using fiber paper

Additional Items

- Stainless steel wave mold - 12" x 20" (30 x 51 cm)

Stainless Steel Wave Mold

This is our stainless steel wave mold without surface preparation. In this photo is set-up with the valley in the middle and the hills on the end. It can be reversed (turned upside down) to have the hill in the middle and the valleys on the ends (as shown on page 63 at top).

This project uses a stainless steel sheet 'wave' mold that consists of two gentle 'valley' curves and one 'hill' curve (or two hills and one valley - depending on which side is up). I love the versatility of this mold. You can create centerpiece-style displays (top photo), or use it to make a freestanding sculpture by standing it on edge (see second photo). You can also combine two or more slumped wave shapes using the 'Screw-It' technique (see Project 4 page 40) to make a multi level tray, a lighted sculptured, or a funky clock to name only a few of the possibilities the imagination can dream up.

Surface Preparation For Stainless Steel

As you know, most molds and kiln shelves require surface preparation to prevent the glass from sticking and stainless is no different. Standard kiln wash will work but it is not so easy to get it to stick to a stainless steel mold. Boron Nitride is a good separator for stainless steel and it seems to stick better than standard shelf primer. We have had good success with it and it is available from most art glass supply outlets. Some fusers recommend heating the mold in your kiln to about 500°F (260°C), then painting the release on the mold while it is still hot. This method is good but you have to work fast.

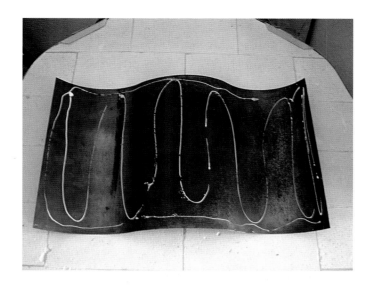

For this wave project however there is an easier way (and you know I like the easy method). Since the mold does not have complex curves we can use the ever-versatile 1/32" (1 mm) thick fiber paper. Cut a piece the size and shape to cover the surface of the wave mold, then use assembly glue to adhere it to the mold. In the photo you can see we have put a couple of items in the valleys (just some things that were handy on our bench) to hold it until the glue dries. I like to sift a layer of kiln wash dust to cover the fiber paper for more protection. If you handle the mold carefully you can make several firings before you would need to replace the fiber paper.

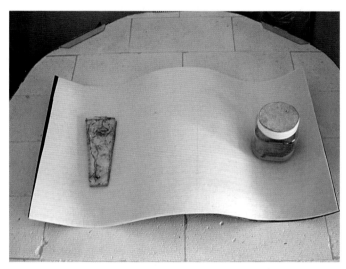

How It's Done

1. I wanted my fused wave to be more of a sculpture that wasn't a standard rectangle and I had an idea to make a trapezoid shape. A scaled down drawing of the pattern shape is shown here at right. The actual size is 9" x 14" (23 x 36) The glass should not be larger than the mold because if it were to slump over the side, it could clench onto the mold and be difficult to remove. I created my full size paper pattern and laid it into the mold to check the size and shape.

3. Set the stainless steel mold aside for now and we'll create the flat blank. Trace the base glass pattern onto a piece of fusing compatible clear glass (non-iridized) and cut it out. Then cut a piece of thin release paper just slightly larger than the base glass.

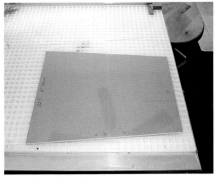

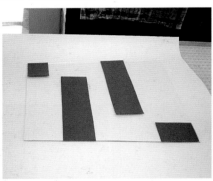

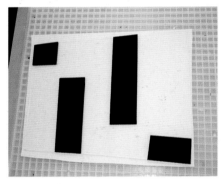

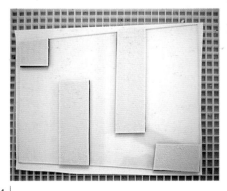

A More Delicate Appearance

4. Now we will add a second decorative layer. Many glass fusers like to work thick, meaning they build up 2, 3, or more layers of glass to create a blank that could be as much as 5/16" (8 mm) thick. I prefer my pieces to be as light as possible, to impart a more delicate, fragile kind of appearance. I have devised several different methods to make my pieces sturdy without adding all the weight. For this 'Airport Gridlock' sculpture I am going to decorate with blocks of black iridescent glass to represent the barriers, then add some vibrant colors of glass frits and powders to signify the mixed emotions of the travelers in the crowd.

5. I wanted to give the colored frit some order and also introduce another decorative option to your fusing repertoire. I cut a few paper rectangle shapes and spent a considerable amount of time adjusting and moving them around until I found the balance I was looking for. I transferred my patterns to the black iridescent glass and cut them out.

Intensify The Iridescent Luster

6. As mentioned on page 51, firing glass with the iridescent side down onto fiber paper intensifies the iridescent luster. This will work if you lay the entire blank (iridescent side down) on a piece of fiber paper to fire it. My idea was to add another dimension by recessing the black glass areas just slightly to catch the viewer's curiosity. I traced my black glass pieces onto a sheet of 1/32" (1 mm) thick fiber paper and cut them out, then glued the fiber paper to the iridescent side of the black glass. Then positioned and glued the black glass to the clear glass base.

7. One other decorative touch was added to this underside before putting it onto the kiln shelf. I carefully positioned and glued a few colored spaghetti stringers around the black pieces. I call this decorating technique 'reverse firing' because it is trapping the stringers and black blocks between the base glass and the kiln shelf. This will create a much sharper line versus the softer line you get when the decorative glass is placed on the topside of a fuse firing.

8. After the glue has set I place my piece of thin release paper on it, then place my KL board kiln shelf on top of the entire assembly. Now hold the clear glass tight to the shelf and turn the whole thing over ready to decorate the topside. If you're not using a lightweight kiln shelf simply use a piece of stiff cardboard to help you turn your glass assembly over.

9. Before decorating with frit we need to add a border of glass around the perimeter for strength and to prevent the black glass from bulging out. Cut a few 1/2" (1.5 mm) wide strips of clear glass, lay them on the top of the base glass to mark and cut them to fit around the black glass, even though the black glass is on the other side! You must have two layers of glass on the edge all the way around. Glue the strips in place and don't overlap them with the black glass.

Painting With Color

10. Frit is available from your glass supplier in dozens of different colors, sizes and shapes from fine glass powder to big glass chunks. You can mix colors and frit sizes to create interesting effects and compelling themes. Think 'painting with color' by applying a thin layer of fine powder for a wisp of color or lay down a thicker layer to intensify the color. I like to first apply my frit with a spoon and then spread it around with a clean paintbrush. If a red particle falls into a blue field of frit simply remove it with a pair of tweezers (or throw a few more red pieces in - artist's choice).

11. When you are satisfied with the decoration of your piece, cover your clay shelf with another piece of fiber paper for even heat distribution (or use a fiberboard shelf). Place the assembly in the kiln and fire it according to: **Schedule C - Large - 1st Full Fuse**, on page 23

12. Clean the fiber paper off the backside of your glass piece in your dunk bucket. Use a fine grit diamond file or an abrasive wet stone to smooth any rough spots along the edge and remove any points that may result from an errant frit or shelf texture. Do a final cleaning to remove grime and finger prints and get ready to drape fire.

13. Place your prepared mold (see step 1) on a shelf in the kiln. Center and balance your pre-fired blank on top of the mold and fire using: **Schedule E - Medium/Large - Drape**, on page 23 to slump-shape your wave form.

The trapezoid shaped flat blank is decorated and ready to be full-fused, flat-fired in my kiln.

> **ProTip**
>
> Some glass fusers assume that they don't have to worry as much about matching the COE of the glass in their projects with the COE of the powders and frits, since they are such tiny particles. But when the frits and powders melt the particles combine to form a skin of glass that will interact adversely with non-matched COE glass. It is important to always match COE's, even when using glass paints. This eliminates the risk of creating unseen tiny cracks that can develop into breaks even years later.

The Wave sculpture after slump firing over the stainless steel wave mold. Shown here free-standing on one edge.

The Frit Factory

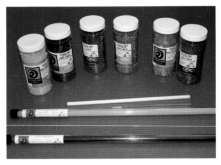

I am fortunate to have a large collection of frits and powders, but occasionally I am unable to find a particular color that I would like to use. Other times I only need a small amount of frit in a unique color to match or contrast with another part of my design. At times like these I simply make my own frit. There are several ways to make frit and you may come up with one of your own. No matter which method you use, please remember to wear your safety glasses at all times!

The Grozer You Get

Anyone who has ever done traditional stained glass knows the value of grozer pliers. They enable you to snip off tiny bits of glass (called grozing) to literally chip away an edge to get the shape you are looking for. In traditional stained glass these bits are swept into the trash but in fusing these bits are renamed 'frit' and become an important design element. One of my students (Frankette) discovered this process quite by accident when she found herself idly playing with her grozers and some glass. It's easy to do, start with any clean piece of glass and hold it over a piece of paper or a tray and move the grozers along an edge biting off small glass bits.

Get Hammered

This method makes frit and relieves frustration at the same time. Simply wrap some smaller chunks of glass, 1" (2.5 cm) or smaller, in a few layers of clean newspaper and then cover the whole thing with an old cloth towel. Take it to a concrete floor (or sidewalk) and hammer away.

The Frit Pounder

You can purchase one of these devices at your fused glass supplier (see 3rd photo from top). It has several different names but they all do the same thing, shatter glass into frit. It works on the same principal as the 'hammer' method but the steel cup contains the flying bits and the plunger does a good job of breaking up the glass. You need to be wary when using a new one of these. We discovered some fine metal residue in the sifted powdered frit after we fired our piece and noticed some black spots after fusing.

The Garbage Disposal

You may have heard of this method, it has become a sort of 'urban legend' in the fusing industry. The idea is to use a kitchen sink type garbage disposal to mass-produce frit. Now don't try this with the disposal you currently have in your sink, you would need to engineer a special rig with running water, a recovery receptacle, a graduated screening system for shifting and sorting and who knows what sort of safety precautions you would need. We've decided to leave the big time frit production to the professionals. When we need a bunch of frit we're happy to buy it ready made.

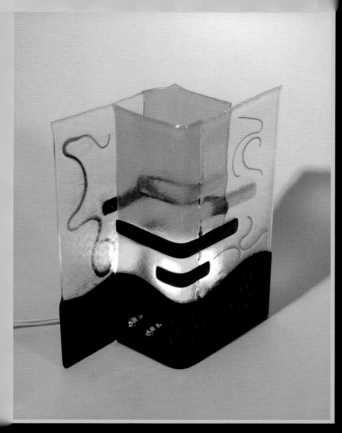

Sculpture by: Shigemi Ohkubo

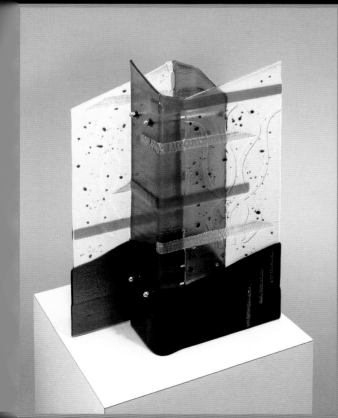

Wall Vase

Glass casting has been going on for thousands of years and has inspired dozens of techniques and approaches. Glass casting is an entire field of study in itself and if you find this little taste intriguing, I would suggest you look into this fascinating field further.

For the purpose of this book we'll define 'kiln casting' as 'heating fragmented glass sufficiently to cause it to flow into a mold (or dam) to produce a slab-glass shape that is thicker than non-dammed fused glass.' Our experience tells us that when standard fusible glass is melted to full-fuse temperature it will flow out to find a thickness of approximately 1/4" to 5/16" (6 to 8 mm) unless a barrier has been placed to stop the flow. That is what we are going to explore here, we will build a refractory barrier (a dam mold) to confine the molten glass and create a cast glass sculpture.

You will find numerous refractory materials available that can be carved, shaped and formed into countless mold shapes. Most casting molds require several steps to produce and will survive anywhere from a single firing to 5 or 6 firings. We want to show you a simple and effective way to create a kiln cast project using KL board for the casting mold. The versatility of this material for casting allows it to be modified and re-used numerous times. We'll take advantage of this feature to make a series of wall vases in different shapes and colors.

Observations & Lessons

- KL board dam molds
- Firing procedures for thicker glass
- Cooling and annealing considerations for thicker glass

Additional Items

- Glass (any COE but all glass must be the same), colors are up to you
- Clear fusing nuggets (optional) see HotTip on page 71
- Stringers for decoration

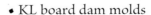
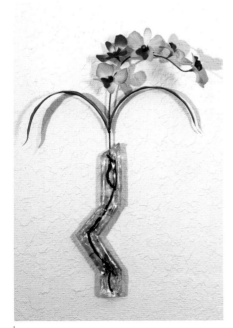

How It's Done

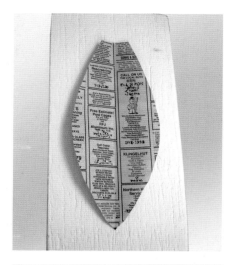

1. To create a casting approximately 5/8" (1.5 cm) thick, use a standard 1" (2.5 cm) thick KL board, with a modified oval cutout shape in the mold. The oval dropout mold that we created for the Lazy Vase project on page 46 could be used or any KL board that you may have with a center cut out shape. It's easy to alter the shape of your mold by adding some pieces of KL board to fit inside the cut out space (See top photo page 20) or you could create a completely new shape.

2. I started with a 6" x 12" (15 x 30 cm) piece of KL board. I wanted to invent a new shape for this project so I folded a few pieces of newspaper in half (a small contribution to the 'reuse & recycle' effort) and cut some shapes (or more precisely - cut half shapes) until I found one that I liked. The shape I created is approximately 4" x 10" (10 x 25 cm) and the cut out will fit inside the sheet of KL board that I have selected. The outside border frame should be at least a 1" (2.5 cm) to give the mold sufficient stability. Then I traced and cut my shape in the center of the board. Remember to save the cutout piece, it could be used as a key segment in a future mold assembly. piece. Now place the new mold on top of another KL board that is about the same size.

Line The Mold With Thin Release Paper

3. The next step is to line the bottom and all edges of the mold with thin release paper. This will give the cast glass a relatively smooth surface. First cut a piece of thin release paper slightly larger than the cutout and place it between the top mold and the bottom board (use a little glue to hold this assembly together). Next line the inside edge of the cut out area with 1" (2.5 cm) strips of thin release paper, overlap the strips and glue them to the mold. You can see in the photograph that I put an additional piece of board in the center of my mold. This is a piece that I had from a previous project and I thought an opening in the center of the vase would add some interest. I placed this small piece in the mold, secured it with a little glue and wrapped it with a strip of thin release paper.

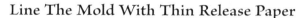

> ### ProTip
>
> We learned the trick of lining the inside edges of the casting mold with strips of thin release paper from one of our students in Las Vegas (thanks Mike). It ensures a clean release and gives the edges a smoother look. I use this method so often now that I've made myself  a strip gauge out of glass. I cut a piece of glass 1" x 12" (2.5 x 30 cm) and ground off the edges. Now when I need release strips for a casting mold, I use my custom strip gauge and a craft knife to make the task effortless.

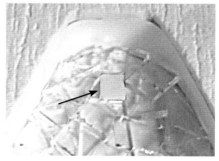

This small square of fiber paper (see arrow) will create a hole to hang the wall vase (see step 4 next page).

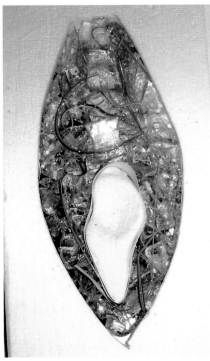

4. Cut 1 piece of 1/8" (3 mm) thick fiber paper 1/2" x 2 1/2" (1.5 x 6 cm) that will be used to create the vessel opening (to hold the silk flower arrangement). Then cut another piece that is a 1/4" (6 mm) square that will be used to create the hanging hole. Glue this small fiber paper square to the thin release paper (inside the mold) near the top edge (see photo on page 69, bottom right).

5. Next prepare the casting fragments. You can use any glass you like, just remember that all glass must be the same COE. The other consideration is the glass should be as clean as possible. Any dirt, grime or foreign particles (like metal shavings etc.) will show up inside your casting. The easiest way to know for sure that the fragmented glass pieces are clean, is to clean the glass before breaking it up. I prefer fragments that are anywhere from 1/4" to 3/4" (6 mm to 2 cm) and I use both my glass cutter & mosaic cutters to make them. Casting is a great way to use up smaller scraps of glass and you can use any colors you want.

Fill The Mold With Fragments

6. OK we're ready to fill the mold with our fragmented glass pieces. In step 4 we created 2 fiber paper pieces. We glued the small square of fiber paper to the thin release paper. Now the other 1/2" x 2 1/2" (1.5 x 6 cm) piece needs to be positioned on top of a layer of fragments to create the vase opening for the silk flowers (I prefer to pick out some bigger pieces of glass for this). Be careful that you do not cover the small square of fiber paper with glass or you'll have to drill out the hanger hole later (see photo on page 69, bottom right). Now position the 1/2" x 2 1/2" (1.5 x 6 cm) fiber paper and glue it to both the small fiber paper square and to the thin release paper on the mold perimeter.

7. Now use your fragmented glass pieces to fill the mold to the top edge of the board. We used mostly clear fragments adding some colored pieces and dichroic to the mix whenever we felt the urge and sometimes we placed casting nuggets in the mix to finish the fill (they add an interesting texture). You can mound the glass up in the center, slightly higher than level with the mold, if you want. When the glass melts down the casting will end up being about 5/8" (1.5 cm) thick, well within the depth of the KL board mold.

8. When the mold is filled and you have added all your decorative touches, place the whole setup in your kiln and fire it according to: **Schedule H - Frit Casting**, on page 23.

Patience in Cooling

One extra piece of advice. You have spent a good deal of time preparing your cast vase and it's going to turn out great if you don't lose patience. You will notice that the anneal soak time for this casting is 120 minutes (2 hours) and the cool down phase has been extended as well. When the kiln has cooled to around 100°F (38°C) I like to wrap the casting (mold and all) in a fiber blanket and leave it inside the kiln for another 24 hours (if you need the kiln for another firing it's OK to take it out but keep it someplace warm). The glass might be cool enough on the outside but it will still be quite hot on the inside. Remember 'patience is a virtue' and a major factor in fusing success.

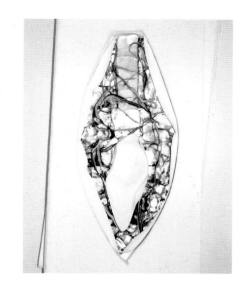

HotTip

Studio nuggets were created for glass blowing, but we wanted to introduce their use in this fusing project. These are available in clear only for 'System 96' glass (COE 96) and are shaped like little pillows of solid glass that are approximately 1/2" x 3/4" x 3/8" thick (1.5 x 2 x 1 cm). They are convenient and easy to use however most castings will require a combination of sheet glass segments and nuggets (as we did in this project).

Hot Streak Bud Vase

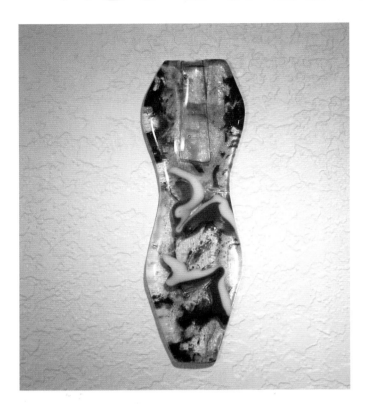

N o doubt you have seen photographs in books or magazines of fused pieces where the colors in the glass are mixed to create a wavy pattern, similar to the one shown in this project. Manipulating (or raking) the molten glass in the kiln while it is very hot creates this wavy pattern. Some fusers call this process combing while others call it raking. The first step is to create a multi-layered blank with a sharply contrasting color design. The glass is then fired to a very high temperature (1650°F / 900°C) to make it soft and pliable enough to be stirred. Then use a special stainless tool, called a rake, to create swirls on the surface.

Observations & Lessons

- Using a KL board dam mold
- Firing temperature for raking
- Discussion of objects that can be raked

Additional Items

- Stainless steel rake

Kiln Types

Our front-loading kiln (shown in the photo at left) is perfectly suited for this technique giving us easy access inside the kiln to manipulate the hot glass. But you can still enjoy great success raking in a top-loading kiln after a simple modification. Use fire bricks that are sufficiently high enough to raise the kiln shelf up into the top section of your kiln (fire bricks are more stable than kiln posts). Position the shelf about 6" (15 cm) down from the top edge of the kiln to eliminate the need to reach way down into the hot kiln to manipulate the glass. The higher shelf also positions the elements (located in the kiln lid) closer to the glass surface, thereby speeding up the reheat time between manipulation sessions.

The Special Rake Tool

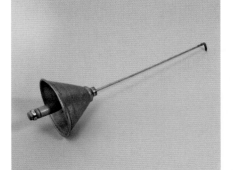

Stainless steel rake tool with heat shield

The stainless steel rake (or comb) is the only special tool required. If you're handy with metal, you could make one yourself using a length of stainless rod but the hook point needs to be just the right size. If it's too thick it draws the heat away and cools the glass too quickly. If it's too thin it will heat up fast and the molten glass will stick to it. Rakes are not expensive so we recommend asking your glass supplier for their recommendation.

Shelf & Mold Preparation

We will be taking the glass up to 1650°F (900°C) and kiln wash will stick to the glass at this higher temperature. This can be eliminated by firing on a KL board shelf that has a layer of thin release paper directly under the glass. If the KL board is uncoated, the bottom of the fired glass will be bumpy due to the texture of the board. Smoothing the fiberboard surface with sandpaper or a piece of glass will greatly reduce this bottom texture. However we still recommend you use a layer of thin release paper on your shelf.

The Raked Vase

We are partial to raking pieces inside a casting mold. Thicker glass has a tendency to spread out at the higher temperature that is required for raking, however when the glass is confined inside a dam mold it's easier to control. The cast vase illustrated here follows the same preparation steps as the Wall Vase Project 10 on page 68, except we've added some contrasting color stringers to the top layer because they really show up well after being raked.

The Rake Firing Process

The firing schedule is almost the same as: **Schedule H - Frit Casting**, on page 23 but the glass needs to be fully heated to 1650°F (900°C). When the glass is hot and ready, put on your kiln gloves and safety glasses, pick up the rake, turn off the kiln (see Safety Note page 74), open the kiln door and rake your piece.

You will have a very short time to rake the glass before it cools and stiffens too much. Simply close the kiln, turn it on, heat it back up to 1650°F (900°C) and rake your piece again.

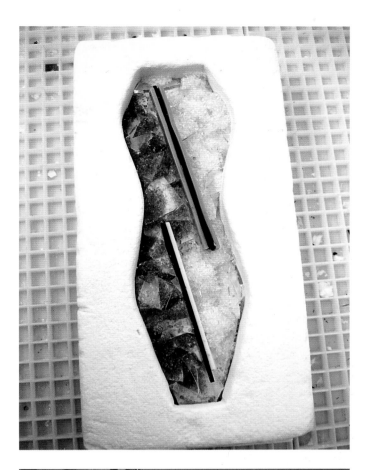

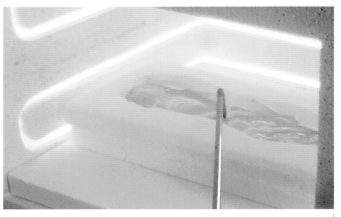

HotTip

As you're raking be very careful to stay away from the mold edges. It's so easy to touch the rake to an edge and knock some release paper or board particles onto the hot glass. Also don't rake so deep that you pull the thin release paper up off the shelf and into the glass. You do have to work quickly but don't be in such a hurry that you risk damaging your piece. Remember, you can reheat the glass and continue to rake it as many times as you like, until you have achieved the effect you are looking for.

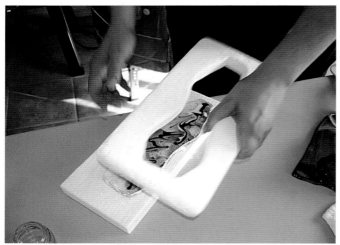

The Raked Plate Special

While it's easier to control thicker glass inside a dam mold, you certainly can rake an object that has not been dammed. For instance, we know that a 3 layer glass object will full fuse to an approximate thickness of 1/4" (6 mm) and from there will not expand or change shape very much. That means you could create a plate or bowl blank with an eye-catching raked pattern. Simply cut the base glass into a disk, a square, or any shape you want sized to fit the slump or dropout mold you intend to use. Then cut a top layer using some interesting colors and decorative components that will really show off a swirling rake design. You may need to do some cold working to grind the edges and the bottom and then fire polish the blank before slumping it into your mold.

This cast penholder was raked during the casting process to create the swirl. Take care when careful when raking a piece like this that you don't disturb the fiber paper insert (for the pen hole).

This piece is actually 2 separate castings, each one fired and raked in its own dam. I haven't decided yet how I will use them. I may place them as a major component in another project.

Raked and Twice Baked Casting

Sometimes I like to put a mixture of colors into a KL casting mold until it is about half full of glass. Since I'm using KL board, I don't even use release paper when I do this! I fire the casting using: **Schedule H - Frit Casting**, on page 23 but I take the temperature up to 1650°F (900°C). I open the door and rake it, close the door to reheat it and rake it again; as many times as I want until I get the effect I like. Once cooled, I pop the casting out of the mold then sandblast the bottom and grind the edges to remove any spikes and clean it thoroughly. Then I line the same KL board mold with thin release paper and half fill it with clear glass fragments. If I'm creating a bud vase or pen holder, I'll position a piece of fiber paper to create the opening (see Project 10 on page 68, step 4). Then place my raked piece on top with the sandblasted side down. Finally fuse fire it using: **Schedule D - Extra Large - 1st Full Fuse**, on page 23 but slow down the initial ramp up speed to 5°F (3°C) per minute, to avoid heat shocking the pre-fused raked piece on the top layer.

You Look Good in Twisted Stripes

Here's a twist for you. The blank we created for the Lazy Vase in Project 5 on page 46 would be a wonderful candidate for raking. Follow steps 3 to 7 (on pages 47 & 48) to make the multi-striped blank. Then fire it using: **Schedule C - Large - 1st Full Fuse**, on page 23, the same one we used in the Lazy Vase project. Only this time take the firing all the way up to the rake temperature of 1650°F (900°C), then open the door and rake the surface. Finish by deep dropping it to create a Lazy Vase or make a shallow dropout bowl using a cutout mold like we did for the fountain bowl on page 51.

Conclusion

Almost any fused piece has the potential to be raked. Depending on the type of mold & shelf release that you're using you may find some embedded fiber particles or baked on kiln wash (see top photo). But these problems can be remedied (by scrubbing or sandblasting) and in the end you will have a fascinating swirl design that is certain to be unique each and every time.

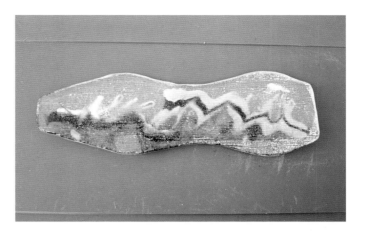

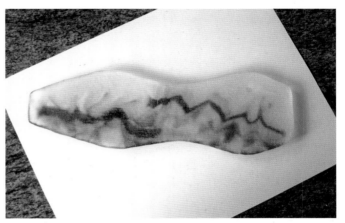

These photos show the bottom side of this casting after firing. The top photo is before cleaning and the lower photo is after the bottom was sandblasted.

This fired blank is actually from the 'Lazy Vase' project that we did on page 46. We used a 'glass-strips-on-edge' method to create that blank and the resulting linear pattern would be a perfect candidate for raking!

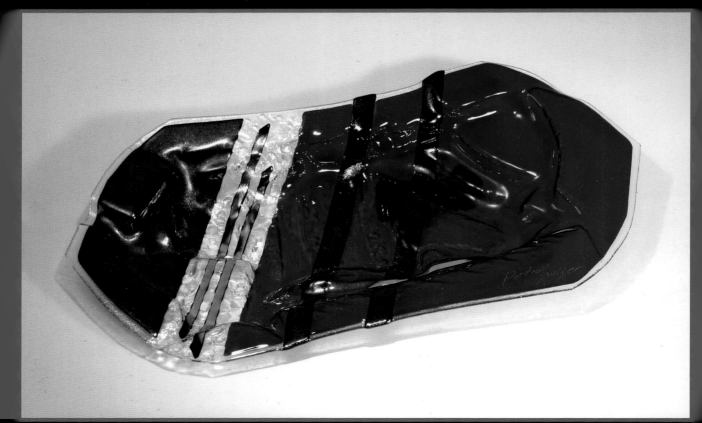

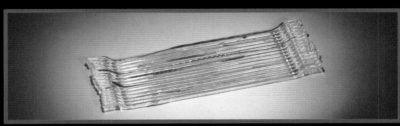

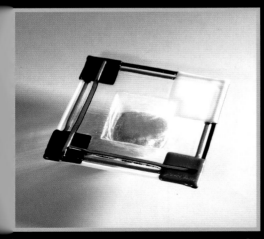

Hors d'oeuvres Anyone?

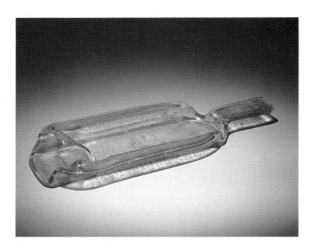

This project will introduce some real world ways to recycle and reuse various types of glass. We'd like to say that our environmental consciousness was at the heart of this effort but we have to be honest and admit that our "frugal" awareness also plays a part. At least one student in every class wants to know if they can work with bottle glass for fusing. So we'll look at the possibilities and challenges of fusing and shaping bottle glass, other food container glass and even window glass. Recycling 'free' glass is alluring but finding ways to reuse or repurpose my broken fused pieces and my stockpile of compatible 'odds & ends' is what really gets me excited.

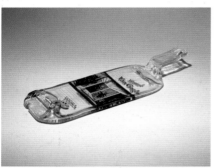

Observations & Lessons

- Turn a wine bottle into a serving tray
- Cast with reclaimed glass
- Decorate with mica powder

Additional Items

- Glass: Wine bottle, Smaller condiment bottles, Perfume bottles, Previously fused glass

How It's Done

Ultimate Recycling - Bottles & Jars

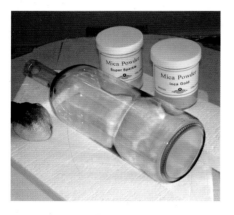

I am sure you have seen them by now - bottles slumped down to make cheese & sushi servers, dresser trays, soap dishes, spoon rests, or wind chimes. Recycling is fun, environmentally friendly and economical to boot. This bottle project uses a standard 1.5 liter wine bottle. It happens to be clear but I also like to fire colored bottles. My favorite thing to do when I'm slumping one of these bottles is to place a piece of KL board under the neck end to create a raised handle. For this clear bottle I put a piece under the neck and also placed 2 pieces of KL board along the sides to create sidewalls on the tray. Since I had some room on the board beside the larger bottle (I hate to waste kiln space) I decided to place 2 smaller bottles that are recycled condiment containers.

These bottles are clear and I didn't want them to be boring so I put some gold mica powder into the large wine bottle and also in one of the condiment bottles. In the other bottle I deposited a few pieces of copper leaf and then stuffed some fiber paper in the top opening to minimize the oxidization the copper leaf.

Decoration Considerations

There are plenty more possibilities to decorate fused bottles, like inserting a dichroic coated paper or color coated paper that needs to be covered with clear glass and is compatible with any COE. Or you can experiment with high fire paints or decorate the project after it has slumped using glass paints that do not have to be fired (a great project for children).

Slump Fuse Firing Schedule for Bottle Glass

Usually I set up one of these bottle slumps when I have a little extra space to fill on the kiln shelf when I'm following a full-fuse schedule such as: **Schedule B - Medium - 1st Full Fuse**, on page 23. I'll adapt for the bottles a bit by ramping the kiln a little slower, perhaps 10°F (6°C) per minute, after that I concentrate my attention on the full-fuse projects and take whatever I get in the bottle slump. Some bottle glass will devitrify during firing and using a clear overglaze can reduce this problem (but it's not fool proof). If devitrification does occur you can still make a nice tray by sandblasting or etching the surface with etching creme after firing.

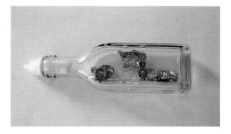

Make Shards - Will Fuse

Casting is another way to use bottle glass, however there are drawbacks. Cast bottle glass lacks the brilliance, shine and artistic possibilities due to the limited décor options. I broke up a dark green wine bottle and used the glass to make the pen holder casting shown in the photo below (back row). It is not a good idea to mix glass from different bottles, especially bottles of different color (due to COE differences). I recommend using only glass from one bottle per casting. If you have to mix glass from other bottles it may work but be prepared for a fractured result.

It's a different story however when you have some fusing glass pieces that may be broken or something that you would like to 're-purpose' in a new firing (we won't discuss why). We had a mishap with a piece and decided to re-use the glass to cast a couple of penholders using the same process as the Wall Vase on page 68. We used 2 different KL board molds for these penholders. Use a piece of pre-fired (recycled) rolled up fiber paper for the pen hole spacer - it will create a round hole for a pen.

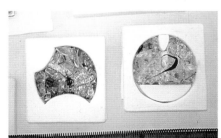

ProTip

There is one little trick to the pen holder. You need to raise the mold and shelf assembly about 3/8" (1 cm) by slipping a piece of board under the top side of the pen holder. (See photo) This will force more glass to flow down into the bottom part of the pen holder making the bottom thicker than the top. This little detail will help them stand up better. After firing give it a little better stability by leveling the bottom on a flat bed grinder.

Pattern Bars & Slices

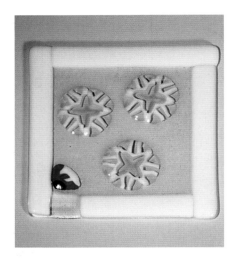

We have introduced a diverse set of projects so far in this book, including jewelry, vases, clocks and even a fountain. The fabrication techniques are quite different for each of these projects but they all have one thing in common - they need an artistic decorative touch to really stand out. You can mix up the colors, add frit or stringers and of course you usually can't go wrong with a splash of dichroic. These are all great ideas for decoration but we like to have the full gamut of options available to satisfy our artistic whim. So lets explore some items (some 'compon-its') that you make ahead of time and have on hand the next time you're looking for that perfect little something that will put the finishing touch on your piece.

Observations & Lessons

- Make Pattern Bars and Colored Rods
- Make Pattern Slices and Millifiorie (using your Pattern Bars)

Additional Items

- Power Tools - diamond blade glass saw, glass grinder

How It's Done

Pattern bar made with yellow cathedral and white opal glass.

Pattern bars and rods are simply assorted colors of glass (usually strips) arranged in a dam mold to create a pattern, then fused together to make an elongated shape. Bars and rods can be made using a single color of glass but these are referred to as 'solid' and we are going to explore the world of 'patterned.' The difference between a bar and a rod is nothing more than the profile shape. Rods are cylindrical (like a pipe) and bars are triangle (as we made here) or square and rectangular.

The use of pattern bars and rods opens up innumerable possibilities for glass fusing. Klaus Moje is a renowned glass artist who has made extensive use of pattern bars in his work. You may have seen examples of his work in several books that feature contemporary fusing artists. A common theme of his requires dozens of thin slices from pattern bars that are laid flat and side-by-side on a base glass (could be colored or clear) to create an entirely unique pattern for a flat fused blank. Different patterns and colors of bars and rods can be mixed in an endless variety of ways. Sometimes Klaus Moje further enhances his piece by raking it (see Project 11 on page 72) or by cutting the blank into sections (after it has cooled), then rearrange the pieces and re-fire the new design to fuse it back together.

Pattern bar slices cut from the bar above and some from a similar bar that we made in red & white.

Pattern Bar Dam Mold

The pattern bar we are creating in this project was placed in a '90° groove' dam mold to create a V shaped bar with a rounded top (about the size of your index finger). The grove was carved in the KL board with a sanding block. We could have carved a round bottom groove in the KL board (using a spoon or round tipped butter knife) to make a 'half moon' shaped bar. Or rather than carve a groove in a board we could have simply placed 2 pieces of KL board 1/2" (1.5 cm) apart to create a square bottom slot allowing us to make a square bar. (See photo bottom right on page 19) Of course you can make the space any width you want and depending on how much glass you add, you could make the bar flat or make it thick enough to build a square shaped bar.

For this V shaped bar we used alternating strips of white opal and yellow cathedral. Each strip was about 1/4" (6 mm) wide and 10" (25 cm) long and one strip was 3/4" (2 cm) wide. We lined the grove with a piece of thin release paper (folded) then laid the strips in the grove to create an interesting pattern. Of course you are not limited to using 1/4" (6 mm) strips. You could place a bundle of spaghetti stringers or several bundles, arranging the colors to form a flower shape (when viewed from the end) or any number of other creative pattern arrangements that you may dream up. Once the strips are arranged the way you want them, cap each end of the mold with a piece of fiberboard, damming the ends of the pattern bar to hold its shape.

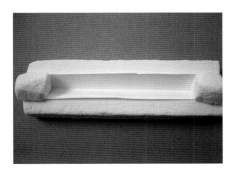

Fire the bar (or better yet set up several different bars and fire them all in the kiln at the same time) according to: **Schedule B - Medium - 1st Full Fuse**, on page 23.

Working with Pattern Bars

Pattern bars are almost always used by slicing them into thin components from 1/8" to 1/4" (3 to 6 mm) to take advantage of the pattern that can only be seen when looking at the profile of a slice. The best way to slice a pattern bar is with a diamond blade glass saw (see photo on page 82, top right). We prefer to use our circular blade 'table saw' but most types of diamond saws will do the job and some of them even have 'slicing' accessories to make the process easier and more accurate. Ask your supplier for their recommendation on saws for pattern bar slicing.

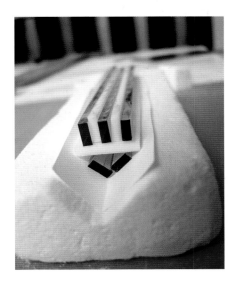

If you created a pattern that resembles a flower, then the resulting slices of that bar are called 'Millefiore' (Italian for thousand flowers). You can purchase commercially produced Millefiore pattern rods that are 1/4" (6 mm) in diameter that can be cut with a glass saw or mosaic shears. You can also buy them pre-sliced. Check if the COE number is the same as the glass you are using on your project.

Ideas for Pattern Bar Slices

We already mentioned one method that artist Klaus Moje uses to design with pattern bar slices. Cut a quantity of 3/16" (5 mm) slices (equal to almost 2 layers of glass) then arrange these slices as the top layer on a colored (or black) base glass. Or simply arrange them on a KL board shelf (with thin release paper) and place the clear glass blank on top of the slices. You must remember to cut the top clear layer into smaller sections or you will trap air under it, causing bubbles to form (unless you want the bubbles of course). Then fire your assembly using: **Schedule C - Large - 1st Full Fuse**, on page 23, to create a flat fused blank. The kiln form the blank into any shape you choose. For example use it for the lazy vase project.

Using a diamond blade table saw to cut pattern bar slices.

If you do not have a diamond blade saw to cut pattern bars, you can make smaller/thinner bars that can be cut with a mosaic cutter. Another way to create a design element is to fire a clear or white glass with a variety frit or powder colors then cut the glass into 'designer strips' after a first full-fuse firing to use it as décor elements in a second firing.

The versatility and potential of designing with pattern bar slices will lead you to discover hundreds of new ways to enhance your fused pieces.

This 'Candy Bar' dish was created using pattern bar chunks that we broke off the bar using mosaic cutters.

Bonus

Here is a Bonus Compon-It for you!

We call these little accent pieces 'appliqué filigree'. A friend of mine has a thing for hearts and he likes to have lots of different sizes, color combinations and sometimes even funky shaped hearts that he likes to use as a kind of signature on many of his fused pieces.

To create your own design, use a craft knife to cut your shape in a piece of 1/8" (3 mm) fiber paper. Unfortunately The fiber paper mold gets too soft to reuse when it's fired so it's only good for a single use. Fill the mold with frit chunks and accent colors.

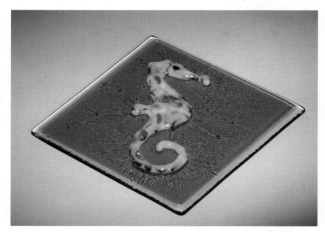

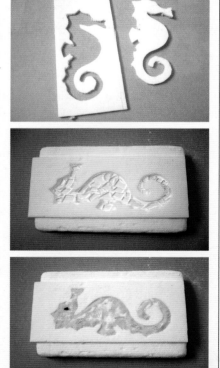

We fused our 'Compone It' shape to a clear base and a little smaller blue iridescent glass. Even in a full fuse firing the sea horse is only tack fused on the tile and the irid glass is pulled in, giving the impression of moving water.

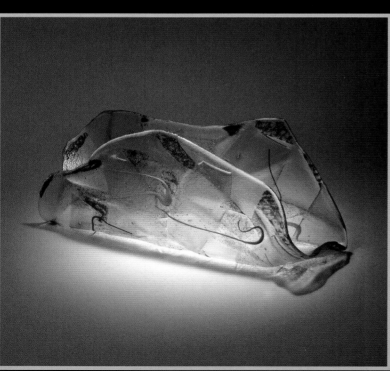

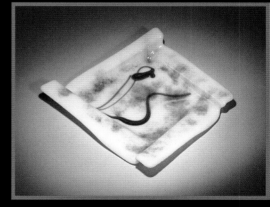

Lesson 15 - Compon-It (Component)
Gestural Strings Of Glass

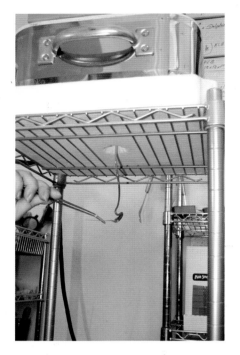

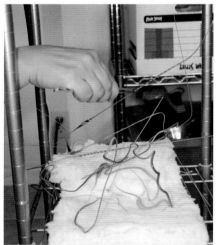

In the mid 1980's Narcissus Quagliata was developing his now famous 'light painting' technique. He was taking part in the Bullseye Glass 'Connections' program looking for a way to create strings of glass that would approximate the gestural quality of brush painting. Rudi Gritsch was the kiln working director at Bullseye Glass at the time and was enlisted to design and build a kiln that could produce these gestural strings of glass. He stacked 3 kiln belt sections and mounted them approximately 72" (1.8 m) high on an 'A' frame ladder rig that he created.

He cut a hole in the floor of the lower kiln and positioned a clay flowerpot over the hole. Then he filled the pot (aka crucible) with broken bits of glass, heated the kiln to melting temperature and when the glass began to leak out the bottom of the kiln he caught it on a metal tray (wearing heat protective gear of course) and moved the tray around to create the gestural strings of glass. This ingenious setup was dubbed the 'Vitrigraph' Kiln ('vitri' is Latin for glass and 'graph' is Greek for writing).

I was fascinated by the possibility of creating those stringers myself and I had to find a way to setup a 'Vitrigraph' device in our studio. We have limited space in our kiln room plus we have students circulating regularly so the ladder style setup would not be very convenient. We considered mounting a shelf about 48" (1.2 m) high on a wall but we really wanted a portable setup, so we could take it with us on remote seminars. Eventually we found the ideal shelving setup at a department store. The top of the shelf is about 14" (35 mm) square and fits the kiln perfectly and the unit sits about 42" (1 m) high .The main requirement for the stand is that it needs to be all metal and the top supporting shelf will need to have a hole drilled in it to allow the molten glass through. Ours had a wire shelf so we cut out a few of the wires in the center area (see photo at top left).

Observations & Lessons

- Setup a 'Vitrigraph' Kiln and rename it 'The Kaiser Lee Glass Flow System'
- Make single and dual colored 'curly' stringers (using the Flow System)

Additional Items

- Terracotta planter pot - 4" (10 cm) top diameter by 4" (10 cm) high
- Metal shelving rack, to support kiln at 42" (1 m) off the floor

Kiln Building

The original Bullseye 'Vitrigraph' kiln consisted of 3 kiln belt sections stacked on top of each other. We wanted to see if we could reduce that number to just one belt section. That way we could use the small portable 'box' kiln that we already had. We replaced the bottom of the kiln with a piece of KL board 2" (5 cm) thick but the 1" (2.5 cm) KL board material will also work. If you plan to mount your kiln on a shelving unit (as we did) be sure to cut the KL board large enough to cover the bottom of your kiln (note: make sure no part of the shelving unit is flammable). Next drill a 3/4" (2 cm) hole in the center of the KL board, then center your terracotta planter pot (the crucible) directly over the hole and trace a line around it onto the board. Now carefully carve a slight depression, about 3/16" (5 mm) deep, into the KL board to accommodate the pot. That's it! Put the whole thing together to make sure it all fits. There should be at least 1/2" (1.5 cm) space between the top edge of the pot and the kiln lid.

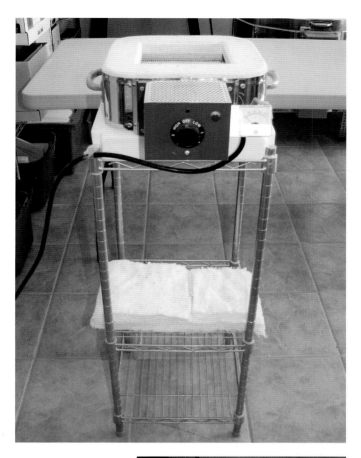

Load the Crucible

1. Any scrap pieces of glass can be used to fill the crucible, just make sure all the glass is the same COE. Single color stringers are very useful and you can make them entirely from the same sheet of glass or mix in some clear glass to thin the color out a bit (an opportunity to use up some clear scrap). Use mosaic cutters to break the glass into pieces from 1/4" to 3/4" (6 mm to 2 cm). You could use even smaller pieces, in fact you can use purchased frit (use the coarse size) if you want, but first cover the hole in the bottom of the pot with a larger piece of compatible glass (clear) to prevent the frit from falling out before it melted.

2. We prefer to fill the crucible outside of the kiln then place the loaded crucible into the kiln. You can fill the pot almost to the top if you choose. Just remember that once the melt starts you will want to keep it going until you have used up all the glass in the pot and you'll be amazed at how many stringers you can make with one pot full. I should mention that we only use the pot for one firing. I suppose it would be possible to use it for more but they as so inexpensive that it is not worth the risk of having the pot break or crack during a second firing and leaking molten glass all over the inside of the our kiln.

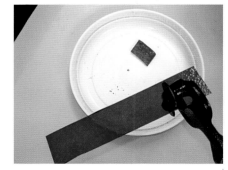

3. One of our favorite projects to make is 'duel colored' stringers. These pieces come out of the pot with a color on one side and a different color on the other side. Duel stringers are created by loading the pot with 2 contrasting colors, separated by a divider. As the striped stringer emerges during the melt you can manipulate it just as you would a single color stringer or give it a twist to make a 'candy cane' style stringer. The secret is to use contrasting color combinations such as red/amber, red/black, blue/lime or white opal/or just about any other color combination.

4. Cut a piece of craft paper to fit snuggly down the center of your terracotta pot, then fill each side with a different color. Here we are using blue and clear on one side of the divider and green and clear on the other side. When you have both sides filled carefully REMOVE the craft paper divider. Originally we thought we needed to make the divider out of steel or clay to be able to leave it in the pot during firing. But as you will see, that is not necessary.

5. Once you have your crucible filled (either with a single color or with duel colors) put it in your kiln. Placing the pot into the depression you made, automatically lines it up with the hole in the KL board kiln bottom. Close the kiln and you are ready to go - almost! **Before turning on the kiln you must have your safety equipment and tools prepared and readily available!** You will need kiln gloves, safety glasses, long tweezers, 2 layers of fiber blanket, an aluminum (or stainless steel) baker's tray, a dunk bucket, and a low stool to sit on. I like to place my tools, the fiber blanket, the dunk bucket and the baker's tray conveniently around the stool.

Fire Up The Kiln

6. It is not necessary to provide a firing chart for this firing. When we first started doing this we ramped up slowly because we did not know how the terracotta pot would react but we found that we could turn our kiln to med-high for ½ hour or until it reached 1000°F (538°C) - that's a 30°F (16°C) per minute ramp speed, then turn it to high until the glass begins to run. Depending on glass type and the speed of your kiln, the glass will begin to flow when the pyrometer is between 1700°F (927°C) and 2000°F (1093°C). DO NOT leave your kiln - even for a minute - after you have turned it on. You do not want to read this headline in your local paper - *'Studio Burns As Molten Glass Pours Out The Bottom Of An Unattended Kiln'*

7. The first glob to emerge will be moving slowly and the end will be about 1/2" (1.5 cm) in diameter. When it is about 4" (10 cm) long, use your long handled tweezers to grasp the end and hold it up to allow the glass flow to catch up. When it's long enough, break it off and bury it between two layers of fiber blanket to let it cool. Then hurry back to grab the stringer again as it continues to flow. Now the fun really starts, I sit on my low stool in front of the kiln, so I can see the glass as it comes out of the kiln bottom (with goggles on of course). I have a high-temp glove on one hand to manipulate the glass and use tweezers in my other hand to hold and shape the strand as it emerges from the kiln.

8. You control the flow and thickness of the strings by adjusting the temperature. Leaving the kiln on the 'hi' setting will eventually make the glass flow so rapidly it will be difficult to control. When this happens simply flash cool the kiln by opening the lid for a few seconds, then close the lid and turn the kiln down to medium high. After a few minutes the flow will slow down too much, just turn it back to hi and keep on going. Soon enough you will develop a rhythm to regulate the temperature range that you like to work within.

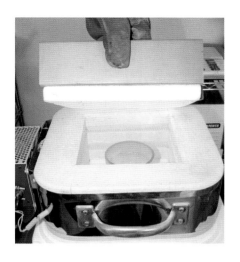

A Gestural Stringer Ballet

9. With a little practice you will be making all sorts of 'gestural stringers.' Here are a few techniques that you can try. Create thick and thin stringers by alternately pulling, waiting, pulling, waiting, as the string descends. Put kinks and bends in the string using your tweezers, pliers or other crimping tools. Wrap the hot string around a metal pipe to make spiral rings. Let the glass get really hot and catch the free-falling string on your tray to create a glass 'birds nest.' Experiment freely and have fun, I'm sure you will discover many creative ways to manipulate your stringers.

10. Most of the stringers that you will make are so thin they do not need to be anneal-cooled in the fiber blanket. However whenever a stringer, or a section of a stringer is 1/4" (6 mm) or larger it is safer to put it in the blanket to let it cool a little slower. When your stringers have cooled sufficiently place them in a storage box that is clearly marked with the COE of the glass you used.

11. All that is left to do is use your new creations to enhance your work. Now that you know what to look for, you will see numerous examples of 'gestural stringers' used in the work throughout this book. The project shown below left uses these stringers as well as the clock on page 40, two of the clocks on page 45 and the Pendant Lights on page 58 to mention only a few.

Here I am holding the hot glass string with my hi-temp glove on my left hand and bending and shaping it with the tweezers in my right hand.

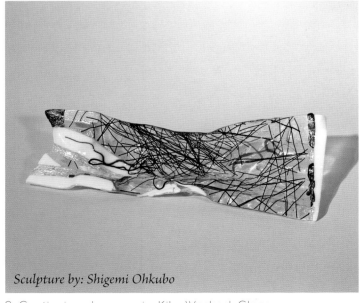

Sculpture by: Shigemi Ohkubo

This aluminum baker's tray holds the bounty of stringers that we created from one pot full of glass. Store them in boxes (shoe boxes work great) with the colors and COE marked on the outside.

Lesson 16 - Sell It
Selling Your Work

When I first started glass fusing I was not even thinking about selling my work. I soon got hooked on the thrill and excitement of opening the kiln the next morning to see my latest work. I couldn't stop myself from creating new and different work and it wasn't long before I had made more items than we could fit into our home or the homes of our friends. On top of that, the cost of glass and supplies really adds up especially when you continue to fill the kiln with new projects. Eventually I decided to investigate the possibility of selling my work. Suffice it to say my experience in that regard has been quite a journey.

First of all I need to mention that there are many fine books on the subject of marketing for arts or crafts. It is not my intention to cover this entire subject in this limited space. I do hope that I inspire you to seek out these books and study them carefully. You will find countless do's and don'ts when it comes to promoting and selling your own work. I can only hope to give you a place to begin your journey with your head and your heart pointed in the right direction.

Get Involved

I joined the South West Florida Craft Guild around the same time that I began to fuse. Membership in that organization has proven to be very helpful. I remember feeling bewildered and disoriented at the first few meetings. I knew a few people but I didn't understand the lingo and I had never exhibited at any of their shows although I had attended some. But that all changed by asking questions whenever I did not understand. People were more than willing to clarify, explain and help me get involved. I've learned so much, met so many new friends and continue to enjoy and benefit from my SWFC Guild connections. I encourage you to seek out and join a Craft Society, Glass Art Guild or a general Art Group in your area. One of their main functions is to organize exhibits, juried shows, lectures and sales events.

Selling your work at a local craft event is a great place to gain some exhibiting and selling experience. There are of course many more opportunities available for you to get your work seen by interested buyers.

Places To Sell Your Work

The following is a list of common art/craft venues and each one has a unique marketing style with positive qualities as well as shortcomings.

- Art and Craft Shows - setup and run your own temporary exhibit tent
- Charity Fund Raisers - you agree to donate a portion of the selling price
- Consignment Shops - purchase goods at discount wholesale price only when the item is sold
- Galleries & Gift Shops - some are consignment, some purchase wholesale
- Guild or Group Showings - are anything from an individual to a multi-artist event
- Personal Functions - a reception & sales event by invitation at your home/studio
- Retail (Reseller) Stores - purchase goods outright at wholesale price
- Studio Showroom - sell direct from your own studio with public store hours
- Web based sales (i.e. E-Bay, Yahoo & others) - to name a few

Establishing A Fair Price

Getting your work in front of many interested buyers is only part of the equation. The object of selling your work is not only to recover your input costs (material and overhead) but also to make some proceeds for your own effort. The amount (percentage) of the proceeds (profit) is a personal choice but the input cost is a cold hard fact that can and should be carefully calculated. Too many artist use a 'seat of the pants' or a 'by-guess-or-by-golly' approach when setting prices and all too often underestimate what the piece needs to sell for in order to simply break even on input costs, with no consideration for the artists own effort. I created a very simple form for myself that I use to help keep track of my projects. I keep a stack of these forms on a clipboard near my workbench and when I start a new piece I also start a new form. The form prompts me to fill in all relevant information about each project - things like the item name, size and description, the date I made it, a list of materials used, both in quantity and cost, number of hours it took to create, any comments about the production, i.e. if an unusual firing or setup was required, how much cold working was needed, etc. I write down everything that could assist me to determine a fair price for the piece. A 'fair price' means fair to the creator (me), fair profit for the distributor (store, museum, show, etc) and a fair price for the final consumer. If any of these links in the marketing chain is weak, the system will break down and nobody wins.

	Title:
	Size &/or Description:
Place Photo of Item Here	Consignment arrangement and considerations:

Date Delivered:		Date Delivered:
Retail Price:		Wholesale Price:

Artist Name & Contact Information:	Store/Gallery Name, Managers Name & Contact Information:

Let's Discuss Consignment Sales

Every venue has positive qualities and shortcomings. I can't describe them all here but I did want to touch on one in particular - 'Consignment Sales.'

It is curious how many owners assume that artists will enthusiastically jump at the chance to consign his or her work. I guess we artists have to take some of the responsibility for this. As emerging artists we may have a tendency to be insecure about our work and are thrilled when a gift shop or gallery shows interest in our work, then suggests a consignment arrangement. I have entered into several consignment deals and have had some consignment sales successes. I have worked with some wonderful gallery store owners who are earnestly trying to help artists make sales. But I have had some experiences that were less than brilliant. There were times my pieces sat in the store for months, collecting dust, until I finally picked them up. Other times my creations were broken, damaged, or just plain missing and I was lucky if I received the broken chunks and a sincere apology.

Displays

One major issue is the lack of appropriate displays for fused work. An elegant bowl placed by itself on a white pedestal that is lit from underneath has an impressive art quality. That same bowl set on a dark unlit shelf in the midst of too many other pieces is dismal and uninspiring. Unfortunately many stores are not experienced or equipped to display art glass pieces in the best light. Even with these drawbacks consigning your work is very often the only choice available to get your work into stores. It's a good idea to be working with more than one store to get a wider audience for your work and to provide an opportunity to exchange your work between venues on a regular schedule.

Accounting & Agreements

It's important to keep careful records of what work is where. You must have a signed agreement between yourself and the venue laying out the consignment undertaking and policy (who does what, when etc.). Then use the form above to record every item to be consigned. Make two copies and when an item is delivered, fill out the details and give one copy to the store and keep the other for your records.

The final word on selling your work. When someone that you do not know purchases one of your pieces, it is truly the ultimate compliment. Your artistic creation was appreciated and admired so much that someone was willing to spend their own hard earned money to possess it. What bigger thrill is there than that?

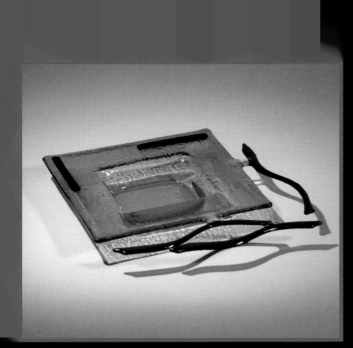
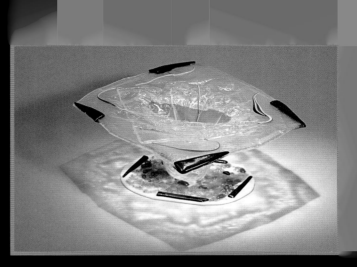

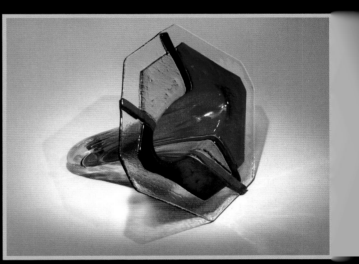
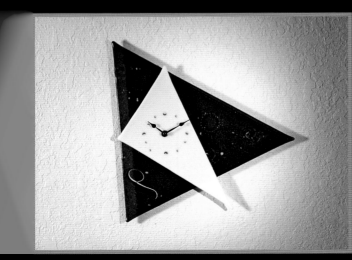
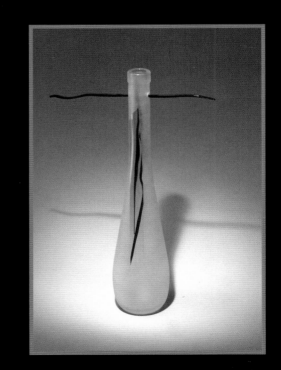

A Party Program

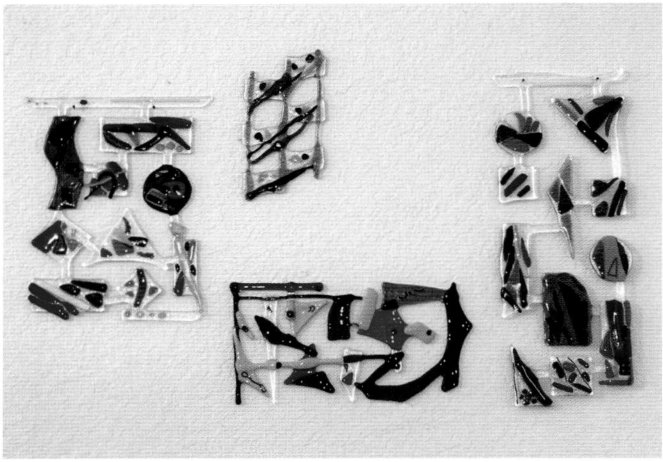

Once a year we have a glass lover's party. Besides food and refreshments, we wanted to add some glass creativity to the party. Since then we have used the same idea at wedding and shower parties, birthday parties, group projects in after school programs, fund-raisers and exhibitions. It always seems to bring people together, start conversations and even friendships.

Observations & Lessons

- How much fun people have creating 'art'
- Adding some fun to any party
- Bringing a new group of people together

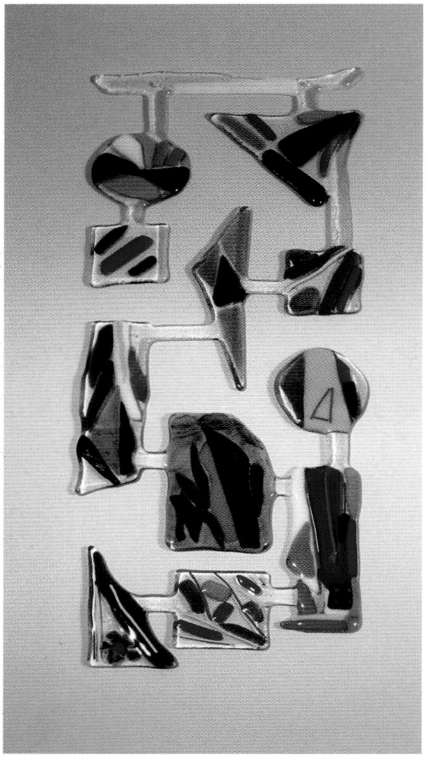

What You'll Need for the Guests

- Glasscutter, Grozer/breaker pliers, Mosaic cutter, Tweezers, Marking pen, Assembly glue, Glass cleaning supplies, Cutting board, Glass gloves
- Beginner book "Introduction to Glass Fusing" by Petra Kaiser, so people can get more information about the art of glass fusing (offer it for sale along with instruction classes if you offer them)
- Plastic trays (recycled foam trays from grocery store)

Provide Glass From Only One COE

- Clear glass precut shapes (for starting bases) - rectangles, squares, triangles, octagons, circles, or random shapes - varying sizes from 2" to 4" (5 to 10 cm). You'll need at least one base piece for each guest you're expecting at the party.
- A tray of assorted colored scrap glass (be sure to include stimulating colors) - smaller pieces are best (less cutting and shaping for guests)
- Stringers, noodles, frit, powder, pattern bar slices, reclaimed pieces, etc.

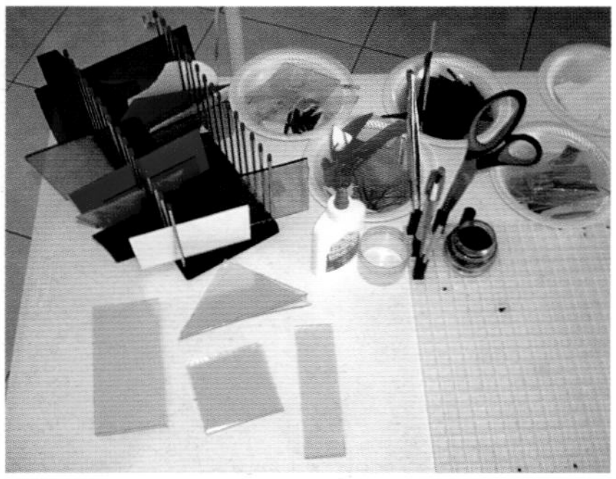

How It's Done

Before any guests arrive gather your tools and supplies and set up a table be used exclusively as the art glass creation station. Create some simple 'tent style' signage to explain the various work-stages. For example, the first sign would be 'Pick a Base Glass' set near the selection of pre-cut shapes. The next work-stage would be 'Select Some Decorative Accents' the next 'Clean and Glue Your Accents To The Base.' The last work-stage is 'Place Your Finish Piece In This Tray,' to keep the pieces together in a holding tray (recycled supermarket foam trays). The final sign will direct them to 'Please Sign The Guest Register' to list their name and e-mail to send a photo of the final fused piece (and perhaps other photos) after the party.

Now all you have to do is make an announcement to your guests, inviting them to 'take a moment to be creative' sometime during the party and explain briefly what you want them to do. You will be amazed how it will get the conversation going. Guests have told me numerous times how much they enjoyed meeting and working with other guests so easily with the help of this project.

After The Party

The next day take the trays full of your guest's creations to your studio. Prepare a kiln shelf, I use a KL board shelf and arrange the guest's pieces on the shelf. Cut a number of 1/2" (1.5 cm) wide clear glass strips and use them as connectors pieces to attach all the guest creation pieces into a single wall or window hanging (see photos on previous page). As a final touch, if you have a ceramic glaze pen (or hi-fire glass enamel), write the date and location of the party on an extra base piece and include it as one of the components as a reminder of the day.

Marketing the Party Program

Party planners are always looking for new ways to entertain guests and this 'Interactive Glass Art Project' could hit the spot! Guests have something fun to do and the hosts will have a piece of art to remind them of a wonderful event and their friends will remember as well when visiting later. Get some experience first by introducing this program at a party of your own. Take plenty of pictures and collect some comments from your guests. Now create a written outline of the program along with a slideshow (on a CD if you want) of the photos from your own party. Calculate a price to set it up, tear down, clean up, fire the piece and deliver it back within a certain period of time. Then send this marketing package to all the party planners in your area.

> **ProTip**
> For an additional charge, you could create a jewelry piece for each guest (something very simple) as a party favor. Or offer to take photos of the guests working on the 'Interactive Glass Art Project' and create a CD slideshow that will be presented to the host when you deliver the finished art piece.

Other marketing possibilities

Sell the 'Interactive Glass Art Project' as a party gift from a guest or a group of guests, presented for a Birthday, Shower, or other special occasion party.

Or use the idea to draw customers to your display table or sales booth at community art show events. We did this at a charity fund-raiser and after the show we gave the finished art piece as a thank you gift to the event organizers.

> *Dear Guests,*
>
> *We invite you to participate in our 'Interactive Glass Art Project' by decorating one piece of glass with a colored design of your own creation. All completed guest pieces will be assembled and fired later in our studio to create a beautiful wall or window ornament to remind our host of this wonderful event and your presence here today.*
>
> *Just follow these 5 easy steps, or ask one of the other guests who has already finished one.*
>
> - *Choose one base glass, you may change the shape*
> - *Ask someone to show you how to cut glass*
> - *Choose some decorative colors*
> - *Clean all your glass pieces*
> - *Glue your accent pieces to the base glass using just a small amount of assembly glue*
>
> *Finally add your name and email address to our guestbook and we will email a picture to you so you can see the finished wall sculpture.*

Lesson 18 - Diagnose It
Troubleshooting

Many readers have told me that they enjoy the three page troubleshooting section in my first book. I couldn't possibly answer every fusing question in 3 pages so it's no surprise that I get additional questions by e-mail from fusers on a regular basis. Those questions help me to formulate some of the HotTips & ProTips in this book and also the troubleshooting questions below.

We've added a troubleshooting section to our website www.kaiserlee.com for your questions and our answers for everyone to read. As the saying goes if one person asks a question, one hundred others are thinking it. So log onto our site and click on the 'More HotTips' button to find out what troubles some of our readers have been getting themselves into - and out of.

Q. You show a beautiful bracelet on page 45 in Introduction to Glass Fusing. I tried to make something similar, embedding loops that I made from 18 gauge sterling silver wire. The problem is that after I full fused the assembly, the silver was black and very brittle. Did I fire it too hot or something? (That 'bracelet' is comparable to the 'Earring Bracelet' project at the top of page 31 in this book).

A. Here is a photo of a spiral ring that I made a while ago. Does the wire look familiar? The problem you (and I) had was with the silver, not the firing temperature. The short answer is, you cannot fire 'sterling silver' wire as an inclusion into glass, however 'fine silver' works wonderfully. Fine silver is 99.9 % silver and it does not turn black when heated. Sterling is an alloy of 92.5% pure silver and 7.5% copper. This mixture gives sterling more strength but it also makes it go black when fired. You probably didn't know that, the thing is I did and I was positive that I had picked out a piece of fine silver for my ring. Unfortunately you cannot distinguish sterling from fine silver by just looking at it. The best way to test if the silver is fine, or sterling, is to heat a piece to melting temperature with a torch. Fine silver will stay silver (white) while sterling will turn black. The other way to tell is to keep your silver supplies well marked so you can easily tell what they are by reading the label.

Q. I tried to make a deep drop vase but the whole thing ended up as a melted puddle on my kiln shelf. Luckily I had put a sheet of thin release paper down beforehand and it didn't ruin my shelf (actually it wasn't luck, I followed your suggestion). It did ruin my vase though. What do you think happened?

A. Either the target temperature you choose was too high or your holding time at target temperature was too long or possibly both of those things happened. When running a deep drop firing it best to go with a target temperature that is around 1265°F (685°C) and let it soak there for as long as it takes. That could be anywhere from 30 minutes to an hour or even longer. I know a fusing artist who creates a lot of these deep drop sculptures and he swears by a target temperature of 1250°C (678°C) and sometimes he has to wait several hours for the drop. He says that this very slow drop technique produces a thicker wall. The bottom line is it takes lots of patience and close observation to create a first-rate deep drop. So resolve to take your time and I wish you better luck with your next one!

Index

Wardell

PUBLICATIONS INC

Instruction, Inspiration and Innovation for the Art Glass Communnity

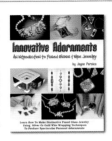
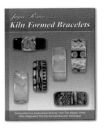

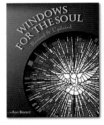

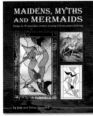

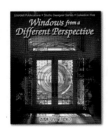
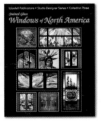

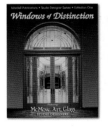

e-mail: info@wardellpublications.com   website: www.wardellpublications.com